Trained first as a physician and now entrusted with the care of souls, the author is uniquely placed to address matters healthy and holy. Providing both diagnosis and cure, he shows how an understanding of God's love for us lays the foundation for loving and being loved.

Alistair Begg
Senior Pastor, Parkside Church, Chagrin Falls, Ohio

This is such a good book! Here is a pastor's heart, rooted deeply in Scripture, informed by careful reading of scholarship, earthed in the realities of the lives of men and women. It is wide-ranging in its scope, balanced in its judgements on uncertain matters, always warm and helpful. I commend it warmly.

Christopher Ash
Writer-in-Residence, Tyndale House,
and former Director of the Cornhill Training Course, London

William Philip is one of our best Bible teachers in the UK, and this is a wonderfully helpful book. Excellent on the biblical text, but also full of warm, pastoral common sense, it will be enormous help to us all in navigating the minefields of relationships. A book to get, read, use, give away and be thankful for!

Paul Levy
Minister, International Presbyterian Church, Ealing, London

Teaching on God's purposes for marriage and relationships is more needed now than ever before. But this book reminds us that there has always been such a need, that the clarity required is found in Scripture, and that it is accessible with the help of a clear and engaging teacher who understands the glories and sinfulness of humanity in equal measure. Here is realistic, relevant and refreshing application of clear biblical truths from an author who knows the grace received in gospel and the mess and angst of daily life.

Peter Dickson
UCCF Team Leader, Scotland

Like focussing a pair of binoculars, William Philip enables us to see further into the wonderful Word of God and the implications this Word has for human relationships. This is a compassionate and courageous book that has both stretched and deepened my understanding of what God intends for our good. I cannot think of a better gift for people today who are being targeted by so many unhelpful ideas than this clear-sighted and compact book on 'Aspects of Love' which God both plans and delivers.

Simon Manchester
Rector, St Thomas Anglican Church, North Sydney

I will be eternally grateful for Willie's clarity of thought, concern for truth, and fatherly care for my husband and I as we navigated friendship, marriage, and the desire for children. As members of the Tron Church we benefited immeasurably from hearing Willie's preaching on these issues. Just as much, we benefited from having a place at Willie and Rebecca's dinner table, where we could discuss how the truth of the scriptures rubs into the grain of every day life. His teaching (and sometimes our shared tears, in the harder times) gave us a greater confidence is the Lord's kindness and wisdom. If you don't have that invite to dinner, this book will serve as an excellent consolation prize!

Caroline Dodds
Member of Edinburgh North Church, Edinburgh

In an age of individualism with the resultant societal crises arising from family and relational breakdown, Dr Philip's book, *Aspects of Love*, based on biblically inspired truths about human relationships, could not be better timed to help people navigate the swirling currents of contemporary political correctness. Those who read it will be strengthened in being light in a darkening world. I heartedly commend it.

Lord Michael Farmer
Businessman, philanthropist and former treasurer of the Conservative Party

At a time of widespread confusion and compromise, here is a warm-hearted, unapologetically biblical guide to navigating the minefield of human relationships. Its refreshing honesty and candid application of the Bible's teaching to the real issues behind a host of contemporary questions make it stand out as a key resource for Christian people, at every stage of life. It will be especially valuable for young people and those who seek to pastor them.

David and Heather Jackman

David was formerly President of the Proclamation Trust & founder-Director of Cornhill Training Course, London

All of us live in a network of relationships that have been affected by the fall. William Philip draws on his experience as doctor, pastor, father and husband not only to give us a diagnosis but also to show us that – through the Holy Spirit – God is working to transform and renew every aspect of our lives. He is changing our relationships and changing us *through* our relationships. This book is accessible, engaging and biblically grounded and I wholeheartedly recommend it.

Philip Stewart

General Practitioner, Suffolk

ASPECTS
of LOVE

OUR MAKER'S DESIGN FOR FRIENDSHIP, LOVE, MARRIAGE AND FAMILY

WILLIAM J. U. PHILIP

TRUTHFOR**LIFE**®

CHRISTIAN
FOCUS

Unless otherwise stated, Scripture quotations are from *The Holy Bible, English Standard Version*, copyright © 2001 by Crossway Bibles, a publishing ministry of Good News Publishers. Used by permission. All rights reserved. ESV Text Edition: 2011.

Scripture quotations marked NIV are taken from the *HOLY BIBLE, NEW INTERNATIONAL VERSION*. NIV*. Copyright ©1973, 1978, 1984 by International Bible Society. Used by permission of Zondervan. All rights reserved.

Scripture quotations marked KJV are taken from the *King James Version*.

paperback ISBN 978-1-5271-0338-2
epub ISBN 978-1-5271-0396-2
mobi ISBN 978-1-5271-0397-9

10 9 8 7 6 5 4 3 2 1

First published in 2019
Reprinted in 2020
by
Christian Focus Publications Ltd,
Geanies House, Fearn, Ross-shire,
IV20 1TW, Great Britain.

with

Truth for Life
P.O. Box 398000
Cleveland, Ohio 44139
truthforlife.org

www.christianfocus.com

Cover and Interior Design by Pete Barnsley (CreativeHoot.com)

Printed in the USA

CONTENTS

For
Rebecca, Joanna and Juliet,
God's great gifts to me,

and in grateful memory
of Ramsay Robb.

Introduction

'All you need is love' – surely one of the most recognisable pop lyrics the world over. First broadcast by the Beatles in June 1967 (the month after I was born) it captured perfectly the heady mood of the Summer of Love, but has endured, no doubt, because its message resonates with our deepest human instinct: we all want – and need – to love and to be loved.

The Bible tells us why this is so: we are made in the image of God, who *is* love (1 John 4:7-8). And, like Him, we are made for the sharing of that love – with Him, and with one another. Love is from God; *we* love because He first loved us (1 John 4:19). Hence – though tragically some realise it only too late – deep down we all know that it is not wealth or power or fame but relationships of real love which are indeed the most precious gift human life affords. Healthy loving is at the very heart of true human flourishing. And the wonderful truth is that because the God of love wants to bless us with love, His words to us are full of instruction about how to love one another – in the truly wholesome (holy) ways which alone can lead us into all the richness and goodness and deep and true satisfaction of love we all long for, and need.

Yet love is an area of human life perennially difficult for many. What is more, today we inhabit a society obsessed by love, sex, romance and marriage, yet more confused than ever about these things. As a result, the very relationships which are most treasured, are often cheapened and devalued in sadly destructive ways. The consequence is much personal unhappiness, family instability, and societal disintegration. Ours is an era becoming defined by the scourge of pornography, the frustration of sexless marriages (surely one of the great ironies of so-called sexual liberation) and the isolation of those increasingly living alone.

Christians are not immune to these pressures; we are human too, and face the temptations common to all. We are also creatures of our time and culture, and much more affected by the atmosphere in which we live than we like to admit. Hence, even the best-taught, most faithful Christian churches must deal with all manner of difficult issues in relationships today.

The truth is that many of us are struggling in all sorts of ways. Some carry the heartbreak of unrequited love, others the pain of strained relationships with children. Many struggle with longing to be married, while others wrestle with marriages under pressure, or live in the sad aftermath of broken marriages. Numerous couples experience the agonies of infertility. Some in our churches endure the pain of children in homosexual relationships, others battle with the temptations of same-sex attraction themselves, and nearly all – whether married or not – struggle with some kind of sexual temptation.

We must be realistic and face up to the fact that there are problems of this nature among Christians. It does not help to pretend it is not so, nor to be too pious to want these issues addressed publicly in church; it is only when we do that people will find they are not alone in their personal struggles, and are encouraged. We have a responsibility to confront these issues together so as to find the help that God's word offers for all of us in these areas of life and love. And it does offer us great help, and also great hope, for all our relationships.

The Bible contains considerable instruction about relationships: about friendship, love, marriage, sex and family, and about the love involved in forming, guarding and keeping them. We need it. Marriage is to be held in honour by *all*, and sexual activity ('the marriage bed') is to be undefiled (Heb. 13:4), so clearly all Christians must be taught how this can be so – whether we happen to be married or single, male or female, old or young. While there is, of course, a place for private counselling and instruction (such as in matters of sexual intimacy), there is much we all need to learn *together*, so that we can help each other to be people with a healthy and a wholesome approach to all our relationships, sexual and otherwise. This is all the more urgent when there is so much unwholesome thinking about these matters all around us, from our parliaments to our playgrounds.

This book seeks to address the basics we all need to know if we are to do that. It began as a teaching series preached to our mixed congregation of different ages, stages and situations, first in 2007, and periodically since, in various revisions. It proved helpful to many (not least in prompting quite a rash of marriages, and a subsequent baby-boom in our church!). I cannot promise this outcome for every reader! However, in seeking to do more than just narrowly equip people for their own marriage, but rather help each of us to understand God's purposes for all our relationships, I do hope that this book will be valuable. For it is as we think through all aspects of love, and above all the divine love reflected in our human love, that we shall truly find the way to healthy loving for holy living.

1. The Foundation of Friendship

We are living in an age of increasing loneliness.

In January 2018 the British Prime Minister appointed what some are calling the UK's first 'minister for loneliness'; the government minister for sport and civil society tasked with leading a group tackling a problem which has reached epidemic proportions, affecting more than nine million adults in the UK.[1] A study by the British Red Cross published in December 2016 found that some 18 percent of the population are often or always lonely, and surprised many with the finding that some of the highest reported rates of loneliness were among the youngest; almost a third of adults under twenty-five feeling often or always lonely.[2]

Not only are these findings terribly sad, they are dangerous. Academic studies have shown the risks that loneliness poses to health. Lonely individuals are more prone to depression, and at higher risk of suicide in older age. They also have greater risk of cognitive decline and one study showed a 64 percent increased risk of developing clinical dementia.[3]

---

1   'May appoints minister to tackle loneliness issues raised by Jo Cox', The Guardian, 16 January 2018.

2   Red Cross report, 'Trapped in a Bubble: an investigation into the triggers for loneliness in the UK', from www.redcross.org.uk, pp. 17-18.

3   https://www.campaigntoendloneliness.org/threat-to-health/ Last accessed 13 December 2018.

We might perhaps expect these detrimental effects on mental health, but loneliness also has an alarming impact on physical health. It increases the risk of high blood pressure, coronary heart disease and stroke, and raises the risk of the onset of disability. The effect of loneliness and social isolation on mortality is as dangerous as obesity, as damaging to health as smoking fifteen cigarettes a day, and overall it increases the likelihood of a premature death by 26 percent.[4]

All this from a lack in something so basic to our human nature: friendship. Friendship is very undervalued in our world today.

God created us for friendship

How wonderful, then, that our God not only knows the need of His people, but delights to bestow friendship; He 'settles the solitary in a home' (Ps. 68:6).

The Bible values friendship deeply. Jesus Himself makes that clear:

> *This is my commandment, that you love one another as I have loved you. Greater love has no one than this, that someone lay down his life for his friends. You are my friends if you do what I command you. No longer do I call you servants, for the servant does not know what his master is doing; but I have called you friends, for all that I have heard from my Father I have made known to you. You did not choose me, but I chose you and appointed you that you should go and bear fruit and that your fruit should abide, so that whatever you ask the Father in my name, he may give it to you. These things I command you, so that you will love one another (John 15:12-17).*

For the Bible, this aspect of love we call friendship is fundamental to our nature as human beings. Humans are not created to be solitary creatures. We are created for friendship, friendship with God and friendship with one another.

That is the picture we have of God and man, as God meant man to be before the Fall; it is also the goal of God's redeeming grace. James reminds us that "'Abraham believed God, and it was counted to him

---

4   Ibid.

as righteousness" – and he was called a friend of God' (James 2:23). As we have seen above, Jesus said to His disciples in the upper room, 'No longer do I call you servants... but I have called you friends'. We are His family, not by the accident of physical birth, but we are a family of His friends. As Psalm 68:5-6 puts it, God is 'Father of the fatherless and protector of widows... God settles the solitary in a home.' God's primary answer to the greatest need of human beings, the need to belong, is this friendship of His own family.

We live in a world where people crave intimacy. That is natural: we are not solitary beings. But our world is totally confused: our culture has confused the need for intimacy with a need for sexual relationships. We think the real, deep, personal relationships of trust and belonging, which we desire and need, come only from sexual relationships. But the Bible says that is not so. It is not marriage that is the answer to loneliness; it is the friendship of real family.

Above all, it is the friendship that comes from true fellowship with God and the family of God. That kind of friendship must be the greatest love of all, because as Paul tells us, this love 'never ends'. 'When the perfect comes', that is God's glorious kingdom, the imperfect, the partial, 'will pass away' (1 Cor. 13:8-10). According to Jesus Himself, that includes sexual relationships. In the glory of the Resurrection there will be no marrying or giving in marriage (Matt. 22:30). But there will still be love. It is the glory of new creation that there we will have the complete intimacy we desire – intimacy, friendship, with God and with one another.

Confusing sex with intimacy

So, the great irony is that we live in a society where there are sexual relationships aplenty, and yet decreasingly little real intimacy. Sex can be empty of real and deep satisfying love. But the Bible says that we can have deep, real and intimate love without sex, and indeed this is the loving intimacy which can endure for eternity.

So we need to think about friendship as an important aspect of love, quite apart from romance or sexual or even family affection. Many relationships involve different aspects of love, and a life-long relationship of marriage will involve many of them. But we must be able to distinguish these different aspects of love.

One of the saddest features, I think, in our culture today is the poverty of real friendships. In the past – and this was true among ancient cultures especially – friendship was exalted as the highest form of love. But Darwinism's legacy of biological reductionism combined with our contemporary sentimentalism about animals leads us to view human beings as just creatures like the rest, and diminishes the sense of man's uniqueness: we are not made as a crown of God's creation; we are no different to dolphins or bats or trees. And at the same time, our culture is extremely individualistic and narcissistic: it is *my* needs as defined by *me* that must be met.

All these things have led to the exaltation of the physical, the urges and the desires that I consider to be natural for me. Hence 'my sexuality' is so exalted. The satisfaction of my perceived sexual and emotional needs has become the most important thing in human relationships. And when we confuse romantic love – sexual love – with friendships, we will assume that all close and intimate relationships must be sexual relationships, whether between the opposite sex or the same sex. If there are deep and meaningful relationships between people of the same sex, nowadays people assume they must be homosexual ones. Twenty years ago, certainly thirty years ago, if two women were to share a house together, nobody would have thought, 'they're probably lesbian'. Today it is the first thing that goes through many people's minds. At the same time, relationships which are not sexual are often devalued and denigrated, so a friendship is not real unless it becomes sexual.

But this has resulted in a poverty in human relationships. Not only are there so many dysfunctional and broken relationships, but there are few real friendships of deep and lasting and meaningful quality. There is a great need in our culture, and also in the church, to rediscover real friendship. And as Christians, of all people, surely we should demonstrate what it means to be a society of friends. We must be real friends, and have real friendships, especially with one another.

So what is real friendship? What does it require?

REAL FRIENDSHIP IS BORN OF A SHARED LOVE

First, real friendship is born of a shared love: love for something outside ourselves and beyond each other. Friendship is born out of a meeting of minds more than a meeting of bodies. It must be *about* something, some shared interest, some passion, some commitment. C. S. Lewis is the most helpful writer I have found on friendship, and he puts it this way, 'Lovers are always talking to one another about their love, friends hardly ever about their friendship. Lovers are normally face to face, absorbed in each other, friends are side by side absorbed in some common interest.'[5] It's something outside of ourselves that binds friends together. It is a shared love, a hobby, music or art or football, or even keeping a special breed of hens.[6]

This interest is not always easy to define. But for real friendship to be possible it must be based on a plane of appreciation of things for their own sake, not the mere gratification of our senses or our certain personal sense of need. It is only through this, not just sharing out of need, which is the basis of real friendship.

That is why, as C. S. Lewis points out, very often people who just desperately want friends, nothing else, cannot seem to make any.[7] The very condition of having friends is that we should want something else besides friends. Real friendship is born out of a shared love for something beyond ourselves, beyond our needs, a shared selfless passion for something else, of someone else. 'Friendship', says Lewis,

---

5   Lewis, C. S., *The Four Loves*, (Collins, 2012), p. 73.

6   One of my good friends has an astonishing array of friendships centred around his devotion to the Wellsummer breed of fowl!

7   Lewis, p. 80.

'must be about something, even if it were only an enthusiasm about dominoes or white mice. Those who have nothing can share nothing, those who are going nowhere can have no fellow-travellers.'[8]

You can see how true that is. Think of two people travelling from one highland village to another. If those are just two locals who are on the bus because they need to get from A to B, it is very likely that they will not be looking out of the windows. They are not looking at the scenery. They do not even notice it: the only thing they are sharing is a seat together on the same bus.

But if, sitting behind them, are two tourists who have come from the depths of the city and have taken that bus purely so that they can look at the beauty of the scenery – the hills and the sky and the sea – they will be talking about it the whole way along. They are taking that journey for the pleasure of sharing the beauty of the scenery; it is something beyond their need for something or for each other. Their shared love of that beauty adds to their friendship.

Sharing love for Christ

So if friendship is born out of shared love, then the nature and the quality of friendship are going to be shaped by the importance of what it is that they share. And for Christians that shared 'something' is a shared love for Christ Himself, a shared desire to love Him and to serve Him. That means that a friendship born out of this shared love, this shared passion, this shared zeal, will be the highest quality of friendship we are capable of.

This kind of ultimate friendship will be quite impossible in an unequal yoking with somebody who is not a fellow lover of Christ. At best, such a friendship will be incomplete and imbalanced. Of course, this does not preclude friendships on many levels with people who are not Christian. But it does mean that you cannot expect the deepest and the most satisfying of intimate friendships with somebody who

---

8   Ibid.

does not share your greatest love, either if they do not share it at all, or if it is not absolutely central for them as it is for you.

This is particularly important to remember before you allow a friendship to develop into a romantic relationship with someone, even if they are a fellow-Christian. It is very easy to fall head-over-heels in love with someone, to be so caught up with gazing face-to-face, with physical attraction and romance, that you do not realise that there actually is not a great deal that binds you together as friends side-by-side. If that is the case, be careful. The first flush of that romantic love will fade in time. So will the second and so will the third, and there will come a time when face-to-face just is not quite so exciting. It is the side-by-side aspect of your relationship that will keep a marriage together when the face-to-face aspect gets a little more saggy! Make sure that you do not find yourself getting into a romance or a marriage where you will discover later on that you do not share very much outside yourselves. Those who have nothing can share nothing; those who are going nowhere can have no fellow-travellers.

Friendship is born of a shared love beyond ourselves, beyond our needs. And we all need real friends like that, especially real Christian friends.

Men need men as Christian friends

In my experience, even in churches, I think women are better at this than men. If I mention a particular woman, and say 'Who are her friends?' usually somebody will immediately say, 'She's really friendly with so and so, and so and so.' Ask that about a man and it is usually not nearly so easy to identify their close friends, and it does seem that men tend to have fewer of those kinds of deep friendships.

There may be all kinds of reasons for this, some of which are simply down to the differences generally between men and women. To say that *Men are from Mars and Women are from Venus* may be a caricature, but research studies have shown that there are significant differences in the way the sexes relate socially. Men's friendships tend to be more practical and less emotional, often based on shared activities (e.g. golfing). In other words, men share activities, women share feelings. Women also tend to invest more in maintaining their friendships, talking more regularly and meeting more frequently, while men do not feel as much need to stay in touch. One study asked men for contact details of very close friends, the kind whom you could ask for help in a tight spot, like a financial loan. They then discovered that some of these had had no contact for many years. In a few cases they had passed away unbeknown to their 'close' friend! So the evidence seems to confirm observations that in general men's friendships tend to be less intimate and less supportive than friendships between women.[9]

But, added to this is something of a crisis in masculinity today. Feminism, with its pressure to minimise, if not obliterate, the sexual distinctives, has put men under pressure to behave in a more 'gender-neutral' way, and increasingly stigmatised the kind of male-only environments and activities where men's friendships have tended to flourish. Greater expectations placed on men in the domestic setting, too, has further focused middle-aged men's time more exclusively around family matters, which, though of course important, may have diminished opportunities for pursuing friendship outside the home or workplace with other men. 'Time out with mates' seems something of a guilty indulgence for the twenty-first-century male.

This is a real problem, and one we must be very careful about in the Christian church. Do not make the mistake of thinking that if you are married then your marriage alone is enough. It is not. Marriage is not designed to meet all our needs for this aspect of love, for friendship. We all need real friends, and for men in particular this may require more deliberate thought and work than we have realised. Men probably have to make more effort and cherish such friendships more than they do.

Married women also need to see the importance of male friendships for their husbands, and encourage their husbands to make and sustain

---

9   Vigil, Jacob M. 'Asymmetries in the friendship preferences and social styles of men and women.' *Human Nature*, 18 (2007), pp. 143-161.

them, not make it harder for them by resenting the shared activities around which men build their friendships. And churches, which often have an array of opportunities for women to fellowship together, need to give serious thought as to how to best develop the kind of activities in which men can grow deepening masculine friendships. Those friendships will bear real spiritual fruit because they are nurtured by a shared love of Christ, and of serving Him together.

REAL FRIENDSHIP FLOURISHES WHEN IT IS SHARED

The second thing to understand is that real friendship is, by its nature, inclusive. As we have seen, there is a lot of confusion in our relationships between romantic love, and friendship. One way that happens is that we can confuse the exclusivity of sexual relationships with the shared inclusivity that is central to real friendship. As C. S. Lewis says,

> *Eros [that is, romantic love] (while it lasts) is necessarily between two only. But two, far from being the necessary number for friendship, is not even the best. And the reason for this is important... if, of three friends (A, B and C), A should die, then B loses not only A but 'A's part in C', while C loses not only A but 'A's part in B'. In each of my friends there is something that only some other friend can fully bring out. By myself, I am not large enough to call the whole man into activity; I want other lights than mine to show all his facets. Now that Charles is dead, I shall never again see Ronald's reaction to a specifically [Charles] joke. Far from having more of Ronald, having him 'to myself' now that Charles is away, I have less of Ronald. Hence true Friendship is the least jealous of loves... For in this love 'to divide is not to take away'... we possess each friend not less but more as the number of those with whom we share him increases. In this friendship exhibits a glorious 'nearness by resemblance' to Heaven itself where the very multitude of the blessed (which no man can number) increases the fruition which each has of God.[10]*

---

10   Lewis, pp. 73-74.

Confusion here often leads to big problems, such as when a romantic relationship, or a marriage, pushes out friends. Sometimes when a natural friendship develops into romantic love (the best way for a relationship to start) it sadly leads to a jealous refusal to share that friendship with others. That is a big mistake. Listen to C. S. Lewis again,

> *If one who was first in the deep and full sense, your Friend, is then gradually or suddenly revealed as also your lover, you will certainly not want to share the beloved's romantic love with any third. But you will have no jealousy at all about sharing the Friendship. Nothing so enriches a romantic love as the discovery that the beloved can deeply, truly and spontaneously enter into Friendship with the Friends you already had: to feel that not only are we two united by erotic love, but we three or four or five are all travellers on the same quest, have all a common vision.* [11]

Losing friendship

But often that is not what happens and it leads to loss of friendships on both sides, and a great deal of real hurt. For example, if two friends become so romantically involved that they begin to forget about and shut out all their other friends, that diminishes not only the friendships but also the romantic relationship. It is less than it could have been. Sometimes there is jealousy in one partner about anything or about anyone else that seems to be competing with their love interest. Usually, this is because one of the two partners is very insecure. They are fearful about losing the affection of their spouse and are confused about what should be exclusive to a marriage (sexual intimacy), and what flourishes by being inclusive, by sharing of our love, by sharing our homes with others.

It also usually means that they are looking to that romance or to that marriage to be the answer to all their needs in life, to be their saviour. They are making their marriage into a god. But marriage is

---

11   Lewis, p. 81.

a god that will never answer those needs. Instead, that jealousy, that desire for total possession of the other person, will wreck a marriage. It is sadly common, and often disastrous, in Christian service when somebody, for instance the wife of a minister, feels jealous in sharing their spouse's time and focus and love with so many other people. They become resentful against those they are serving. That can be terribly damaging.

Here are a couple of tests about this in your own relationship, if you are married, or heading that way. How do you feel as a husband or wife, or as a dating couple, in company with others? Do you wish all the time that you were together and others were not there? Or do you thrive on sharing your friendship together as a couple with others? The answer will be telling.

Another test. Ask your friends: How do they feel being around you as a couple? Do they feel awkward? Do they feel like a bit of a lemon all the time? Do they feel that the vibes you are giving out are that you wish they would clear off? Those are bad signs. That is why the Bible is full of commands not to be exclusive in the wrong way about our marriages or our home lives in particular - as we will see in later chapters.

I always tell couples preparing for marriage that they need to be very clear not to confuse their bedroom door with their front door. A healthy, Christian marriage must have a closed bedroom door to keep all others firmly out – no sharing the marriage bed – but an open front door, to invite others warmly in to share their married home-life in generous friendship.

Think of all the biblical commands to have open homes, to be hospitable, to do it without grumbling, to be involving others in your lives! Shared lives, shared fellowship is the call. This responsibility is especially important in any church for those who are married, or connected to others, to think about people who are single, people who do not perhaps have nuclear families nearby (or at all) or who are single parents, or widowed, or who are lonely for a host of reasons. Our

God is a God who sets the solitary in a home, and our friendships and our marriages will flourish when we share them in the way God means us to share them. Friendship is by its nature, inclusive.

REAL FRIENDSHIP CREATES UNIQUE BONDS

At the same time, friendship is by nature also exclusive, and that is something I think calls for both celebration and care. Despite what I have already said about the inclusive, shared nature of friendship, by its nature real friendship is still something which inevitably belongs within a group. There is a certain exclusiveness that is necessary to real friendship. The Lord Jesus had His special twelve disciples and within that group He had His special three, Peter, James and John. Paul, too, had his inner associates in mission, and special ones like Timothy, who he called his 'son' (Phil. 2:22), and Luke, 'our dear friend' (Col. 4:14, NIV). David, in his struggle for the kingship of Israel, had his mighty men, and so on.

Similarly, when we know something of the preciousness of deep friendships that last for many years, it binds us together; it is a cause for real thanksgiving. In Christian ministry, especially, it is invaluable.

A band of brothers

For me personally, it has been essential to have a band of brothers, who really would die in the trenches with me and for me. Over the years, I thank God that I have had friends whose loyalty I have been able to rely on 'through many dangers, toils and snares'. With them I have been able to weather the storms in church life which might have otherwise washed me overboard.

Some years back, along with others, I had to face a deeply traumatic crisis in ministry. In order to do what we believed essential to remain true to the biblical gospel, a breach of fellowship with others became unavoidable, which was very painful in itself for all involved, but in addition involved ejection from much-loved buildings, homes, confiscation of resources and, for some, false accusations and hostile court actions amid very distressing publicity. But the bonds forged between many of us through those intensely difficult days of adversity are such that 'we few, we happy few, we band of brothers' now share something which has bound us together in a unique way ever since, and will do 'from this day to the ending of the world'.[12] Bonds forged in blood are the deepest of them all.

These unique bonds of Christian friendship are a great gift of God, a creative force, which is part of God's purpose for us. I think for students, particularly, the time at university can be extraordinarily formative, not least in forging deep and real friendships with other Christians which will last a lifetime. Many of my closest friends today are those who go back to my student days. But the same is also true of being part of a church fellowship, where there is opportunity to grow close to others, as you serve alongside them, as you share a common vision, a common passion. C. S. Lewis again:

> *For a Christian, there are, strictly speaking, no chances. A secret Master of Ceremonies has been at work. Christ, who said to the disciples, 'You have not chosen me, but I have chosen you,' can truly say to every group of Christian friends, 'You have not chosen one another but I have chosen you for one another.' The friendship is not a reward for our discrimination and good taste in finding one another out. It is the instrument by which God reveals to each the beauties of all the others... They are, like all beauties, derived from Him and then, in a good Friendship, increased by Him through the Friendship itself, so that it is His instrument for creating as well as revealing.[13]*

God gives us friendship, especially real Christian friendship, as a creative thing, so that we can enrich one another's lives. That is a cause for celebration. But we must also see that the preciousness of what binds us together is also, by its nature, that which excludes other

---

12 Shakespeare, William, *Henry V*, Act IV, Scene 3.

13 Lewis, p.108.

people. There are natural limits to the deep shared bonds between a group of special friends. So there also needs to be care, care lest that unavoidable exclusiveness becomes *exclusivist*.

Exclusivist cliques

It is very easy in a church, or a University Christian Union, or in many other situations for cliques to form. They become exclusivist, where there is a sharing of in-jokes and knowing looks from insiders and a bit of a cold shoulder to outsiders. It may be unconscious (though sometimes, sadly, it is more conscious) but regardless it is very off-putting to newcomers. The corporate 'body-language' of the group gives out a message which powerfully counteracts the gospel welcome their words aspire to convey. Larger churches or CUs may have many such cliques, smaller ones often just one 'in crowd'. In each case Christian groups need to strive hard against this powerful anti-evangelistic force they are prone to.

Paul makes this point forcefully to the Corinthian church, where there was a powerful culture of superiority and exclusivism in the church, centred much around a prideful focus on spiritual gifts, particularly the use of words and speech. In 1 Corinthians 13-14, he sharply rebukes a selfish insistence on inappropriately speaking in unintelligible tongues in their meetings. Instead of lovingly building up the church it was just puffing up individual 'insider' pride; moreover, it was making outsiders and even some insiders feel excluded, so it was wrong, says Paul.

So friends must be careful; it is easy for that exclusivist pride to begin to develop in a group of friends. It is easy to see it in others' friends, but not so easy to see it in yourself and your own group. But it is especially true as believers, because our faith and our love for Christ necessarily separate us from others. It cannot be otherwise, because the gospel excludes unbelief. But ours must be a separation that invites in, not a partition that keeps out. We are not to be like the Pharisees who shut the gate of heaven to others, though they did not even enter it themselves. Nor are we to be people who have no thought for the outsider, either in our friendships or in our churches.

We must be careful in case the gifts of friendship that God gives us, and which we celebrate, give rise to pride. But we can celebrate the deep and the precious bonds that so enrich our lives in the friends God gives us.

WHAT FRIENDSHIP DEMANDS

Fortunately, the Bible gives us clear wisdom about friendship, about its demands and responsibilities. It makes it clear that real fellowship, demands three things: **constancy, candour and Christlikeness.**

Constancy

In the book of Proverbs particularly, we have real wisdom and insight on things that are true of all friendships, but especially for believers. So here is the first: real friendship means constancy and commitment, especially when friends are in pain and suffering.

Proverbs 17:17: 'A friend loves at all times, a brother is born for adversity' and Proverbs 18:24: 'A man of many companions may come to ruin, but there is a friend who sticks closer than a brother'. That constancy is what marks true friendship, in contrast to the false friends that Proverbs also describes. Proverbs 19:4, 'Wealth brings many new friends, but a poor man is deserted by his friend' or verse 6, 'Many seek the favour of a generous man, and everyone is a friend to a man who gives gifts.'

It is not the good times but the bad that show us who our true friends really are. The Bible gives many examples. It can be times when you find yourself out of favour in Christian circles as Paul was when he was imprisoned. It is astonishing that 2 Timothy 1:15 tells us that he had been deserted by all in Asia; every church where he had converted them and served them and taught them had turned their backs on Paul when he was imprisoned. 'But', says Paul, 'Onesiphorus... was not ashamed of my chains,' unashamed of a man who was despised for his faithfulness to the gospel. Onesiphorus' name is known all over the world today, written in scripture, because he was a real friend to Paul. That is real friendship: loving those who are out of favour even in Christian circles, because they are in the dog house with the world for their Christian testimony.

There is also a great need for constancy when friends are cast down or exhausted or discouraged. I have often wondered if God put Priscilla and Aquila into the city of Corinth (Acts 18:2-3) just so that they would be there to refresh Paul in the midst of a difficult and discouraging missionary journey, for him to find people of his own trade, tentmaking, people he became deep friends with.

Constancy can be challenging

It is not easy to support friends when they are really discouraged. It is very hard sometimes to support friends when they are deeply distressed and even ill with depression. It is easy to drop those friends, to move on, but a real friend is constant. A brother is born for adversity. Sometimes it is help in times of physical danger; Paul tells us in Romans 16 that Priscilla and Aquila 'risked their necks for me' (Rom. 16:4), risked their own lives – that is a real test of friendship.

I wonder how constant we really are as friends? Are we sometimes rather mercenary as those other Proverbs suggest? 'All a poor man's brothers hate him; how much more do his friends go far from him! He pursues them with words, but does not have them' (Prov. 19:7). Sometimes that happens when a friend seems to desert the Lord altogether, maybe it's in despair at something that they've done. Job says, 'A despairing man should have the devotion of his friends, even though he forsakes the fear of the Almighty' (Job 6:14, NIV). That was the most unthinkable thing possible – apostasy from God – but real friends, says Job, remain devoted even then. How much more, when a Christian brother or sister is caught in a sin, as Paul says in Galatians 6:1, should real friends be involved to help restore them gently. Real friends will be there when the chips are down – regardless. Yet not like Job's friends, not making a great show of their faithfulness, a great show of needing to be needed – perhaps even secretly revelling in the sort of status it gives them. No, as C. S. Lewis says, 'The mark of perfect friendship is not that help will be given when the pinch comes (of course it will) but that, having been given, it makes no difference at all. It was a distraction'.[14] Real friendship gives no sense of making someone feel a sense of obligation and debt to your friendship.

I hope that describes our Christian friendships. Yet someone I know who once spent time in prison has said to me that he often felt he found more loyalty and constancy among fellow-convicts in prison than among the Christians in the church in which he was now serving. That is pretty damning, is it not?

Candour

Real friendship, according to the Bible, demands constancy with commitment, especially to friends who are in pain. And, says the Bible, it demands candour, but candour with care in being willing to bring pain to a friend. Proverbs 27:6, 'Faithful are the wounds of a friend; profuse are the kisses of an enemy' and verse 9, 'Oil and perfume make the heart glad, and the sweetness of a friend comes from his earnest counsel,' even, that is, when the earnest counsel is not what you particularly wanted to hear.

It can hurt to be honest, but sometimes a real friend must speak truth that causes pain, in order to save a friend from worse pain and even from danger. If you discovered that your friend's wife was having an affair and that she and her lover were planning to murder your friend and run off with the insurance money, you would not say, 'I'm not going to tell him because it will be so devastating for him'. An exaggerated scenario (I hope!), but there are plenty of lesser situations where we might be tempted to seek to excuse ourselves from 'interfering in something that is not our business'. What about a

14 Lewis, p. 84.

friend or family member whose fiancé is known to you to be habitually unfaithful sexually, and you know that they are still sleeping around with the wedding just around the corner? I know of marriages tragically blighted from the start in that way, with immense pain and heartbreak endured, because no-one was honest enough to speak the truth in love to their friend before the wedding. Presumably they did not want to bear the cost of having to inflict pain.

Similarly, I think of some in training for ministry whose personality and temperament – and sometimes behaviour – should have made it clear to anyone with an understanding of church ministry life that it would be far from wise, or indeed kind, to allow them to continue into a pastoral situation. But very rarely is that nettle grasped. All too often the result has been a car crash in ministry, and often in marriage, some years down the road, wreaking havoc on both families and church families alike.

By contrast, I can think of occasions when responsible leaders have been willing to bear the pain – and often severe reproach – of doing the kind and protective thing, in gently insisting on a change of course for such a person. They have told them with candour, though with great care, that this path must be closed to them, and that it cannot be right or good for them and their family life or their spiritual life, to pursue that ministry further. In doing so they have often been wounded themselves, even as they have had to inflict a wound as a faithful friend. But I know that marriages, and ministries, have been saved by such loving and true friendship.

Faithful wounds

Sometimes a real friend, in order to be faithful, must inflict wounds like God does – 'I wound and I heal' (Deut. 32:39). But we need care, great care, because we are not God. Nor is every home truth ours to convey to everybody. There is a time to speak but there is a time to be silent. And there is a way to speak. The Lord Jesus knew how to wound and how to heal, but a bruised reed He never crushed, a smoking wick

He never quenched (see Isa. 42:3). He had perfect sensitivity but, of course, the trouble is we do not. Nor are we infallible. Faithful wounds are not inflicted frivolously or foolishly or, without long, hard heart-searching. Otherwise, great damage can be done.

When I was at university, there were some ultra-pious Christian students who were great believers in what they called 'confrontational friendship'. There was a lot of pious talk, about genuine honesty about sin and so on, but the reality was that, predictably, a huge amount of relational damage was done as they went around mercilessly attacking all their friends for every tiny little fault. Those are not faithful wounds.

Of course, there is the opposite danger that we ignore all sorts of damaging behaviour in our friends, because it is too hard for us to confront. The consequences of that can be equally disastrous, as I have said. Read the beginning of the book of 1 Kings, and you see how David's failure to confront the wrongdoing in his sons, Absalom and then Adonijah, led to disaster for his family, indeed for the whole nation.

A good test, I think, of a right attitude is to ask yourself, do you in any way feel an eagerness to correct your friend on this matter? Do you in any way feel satisfied confronting your friend about something? If you do, then you are probably not the person to speak to them, or it is not the time. But if you find yourself agonising about it, desperate to do anything other than talk to your friend, longing that somebody else would do this, then very probably now is the time, and you are the person and God is laying that burden of responsibility upon you.

It should never feel easy, or make you happy, to speak words which you know will cause real pain and distress, even though they are things which cannot be avoided and must be spoken of. One thinks of the story of Robert Murray McCheyne asking Andrew Bonar what he had been preaching on, and Andrew Bonar replying that he had been preaching on hell. McCheyne said to him, 'Were you able to preach it *with tenderness?'*[15] Real friendship demands candour, with care. Very often that care will require great tenderness, deep heart-searching, and even tears.

Christ-likeness

Real friendship also demands costly Christ-likeness. We must bear pain *with* friends and *for* friends and also, sadly, *from* friends. True Christian friendship is shaped by the cross. It shares and it reflects the friendship of Christ Himself.

We easily misunderstand this. There is a wholly *wrong* way of thinking of our friendship as Christ-like. Sometimes we think that we, as friends, can and should fix every problem for our friends, when they are in a mess: when they are ill, when they are perhaps very depressed, or whatever it might be. But just as we must not seek *our* salvation from friendships or relationships or marriages, we cannot *provide* salvation for others in these relationships either – we are not the Lord Jesus. One of my most frequent quotes to ministers in training (and to myself) comes from William Still's little book *The Work of the Pastor:* 'Some meddling ministers want to sort out everybody. God is not so optimistic.'[16] That is a life-saving message for anyone involved in Christian service! You cannot fix everything in your friends' lives. You are *not* the Christ.

But Christ-like friendship does mean that our love for our friends will often have to bear many things *with* them and even bear a lot of pain *from* them, from those who are or were our friends. Paul says, real love 'is patient and kind... Love bears all things... endures all things; love never ends' (1 Cor. 13:4-8). Bearing pain is a big part of the cost of real friendship because the people who give us the highest pleasure and happiness in life are also able to inflict on us the greatest pain. Often that means our closest friends and family.

---

15   Bonar, Andrew, *Memoir & Remains of Robert Murray M'Cheyne* (Banner Of Truth, 1966), p. 43.

16   Still, William, *The Work of the Pastor*, (Christian Focus, 2001) p. 44.

Real loving risks real heartbreak

Real friendship and love involve a giving of ourselves that makes us vulnerable, vulnerable to hurt. The truth is that often the deepest hurts in our Christian walk come from other Christians, people that we have been close to, people who worked side by side with us in Christian service and ministry. Just read the Psalms – 'All who hate me whisper together about me... Even my *close friend* in whom I trusted, who ate my bread, has lifted his heel against me' (Ps. 41:7-9). Or Psalm 55:12-14, 'For it is not an enemy who taunts me – then I could bear it; it is not an adversary who deals insolently with me – then I could hide from him. But it is you... my *companion*, my *familiar friend*. We used to take sweet counsel together; within God's house we walked in the throng.' It is shocking, is it not, to read that? But we know it is true, especially in Christian life and in service: the deepest wounds, the deepest hurts, will often be inflicted by those we have been close to as fellow-believers and friends - that can make our wounds so much more painful.

The great danger is that, having been hurt like this, we will want to protect ourselves in the future. We feel unable to give ourselves in that way again to anybody in any relationship, in any ministry, in any service, lest the same thing happen again. 'I gave them everything, I gave them my all, and look, look what's happened to me, look what they've done! I can never let that happen again.' It is natural, but we need to beware; that natural tendency to self-preservation and self-protection will lead, if we do not stop it, to a growing coldness and hardness and bitterness in our hearts which will become ultimately irrecoverable.

A penultimate quote from C. S. Lewis:

There is no safe investment. To love at all is to be vulnerable. Love anything and your heart will certainly be wrung and possibly be broken. If you want to make sure of keeping it intact, you must give your heart to no one, not even to an animal. Wrap it carefully around with hobbies and little luxuries; avoid all entanglements; lock it up safe in the casket or coffin of your selfishness. But in that casket, safe, dark, motionless, airless, it will change. It will not be broken; it will become unbreakable, impenetrable, irredeemable. The alternative to tragedy, or at least to the risk of tragedy, is damnation. The only place outside of Heaven when you can be perfectly safe from all the dangers and perturbations of love is Hell.[17]

Where there is real friendship and real love, there must be the risk of pain and heartbreak. In this world of fallen humanity, that risk is a virtual certainty.

But for believers there is another dimension altogether in this Christ-shaped friendship and love. We can never forget the great principle of resurrection, of new life that comes through suffering and death. 'We shall draw nearer to God, not by trying to avoid the sufferings inherent in all loves', says Lewis, 'but by accepting them and offering them to Him; throwing away all defensive armour.'[18] Sometimes our hearts are broken for a reason; that is the nature of God's strange, but merciful, providence. Sometimes it is because we will draw nearer to Christ through that than we could any other way – it is a path that just has to be for our life.

The way of the cross

Costly Christ-likeness in all our life and in all our friendships: that is the way of the cross. That is the way of discipleship. It is the way of witness to what true friendship really is, both to our fellow-believers and to a world that is watching the church of Jesus Christ. The supreme character of real friends is that we bear all things, that we love one another, that we forgive one another, and that we go on loving one another without counting the cost.

I am sure that we all long for these kinds of friendships. The Bible says to us: Do not bemoan your lack of such friends, determine instead to *be* such a friend to many – a friend marked by real constancy with

17 Lewis, p. 147.
18 Lewis, p. 148.

commitment, by candour with real care, and by Christ-likeness with real cost. Proverbs 22:11 says, 'He who loves purity of heart, and whose speech is gracious, will have the king as his friend'. That is how attractive he will be to others. 'I have called you friends,' said Jesus, 'and this is my commandment, that you love one another as I have loved you' – as I have befriended you (John 15:15,12).

2. The Reason for Marriage

If friendship is the way God provides the real *intimacy* we need; if this – not marriage – is His answer to our basic need to love and be loved, then we need to ask: what is the reason for marriage? If sexual expression is not necessary for intimacy in relationships, and the true solution for solitude is the friendship and deep sense of belonging found in Christian fellowship and family, then what is the purpose of the sexual relationship God has given to humankind? What is God's reason and purpose for marriage?

Jesus Himself gives us the answer, in Matthew chapter 19:

> *And Pharisees came up to him and tested him by asking, 'Is it lawful to divorce one's wife for any cause?' He answered, 'Have you not read that he who created them from the beginning made them male and female, and said, "Therefore a man shall leave his father and his mother and hold fast to his wife, and the two shall become one flesh"? So they are no longer two but one flesh. What therefore God has joined together, let not man separate'* (Matt. 19:3-6).

Notice that when Jesus is asked about divorce, He immediately moves the conversation instead to the subject of marriage itself. He answers His accusers' question in terms of the purpose and place of marriage within God's story: the story of God's kingdom from Creation right through to New Creation ('the new world' as He calls it in 19:28). There are two fundamental truths which Jesus makes very clear here: marriage is *from* God – it is a gift that God bestows upon human beings as His servants – and secondly, that marriage is *for* God – it is a gift to be used for God's service and the service of His kingdom. Before we explore these two vital truths, though, we must also see that Jesus makes it very clear that marriage, as He describes it, is defined as the lifelong union of one man and one woman in an exclusive sexual partnership.

Confusion about marriage

The fact that we should need to highlight this tells its own story, and reminds us that we live in an age of great confusion about marriage and sexuality. This is both damaging to society and dangerous for the church, so it is vital that followers of Jesus are clear what He and His apostles teach about what marriage really is, and is not, all about. This is important for all Christians, not just married people, since marriage must be held in honour by all (Heb. 13:4); hence the New Testament letters speak very openly about marriage and sex to whole congregations, expecting the words to be heard by the young and the old, by the married and the unmarried, by male and female. All of us need to understand these things. The New Testament church needed clear instruction about marriage and sex, and so do we – not only because of confusion from the world outside, but also because of corruption within our own hearts. We must be realistic about these things; sexuality is a difficult area of life for almost everyone. Here, just as everywhere else, the church is a convalescent ward in which we are all in recovery: from our sin, and from the consequences of our sin.

That is a very sobering truth, yet also very wonderful. Think of what the apostle Paul said to the church in Corinth, a culture full of sexual immorality, of adulterers, those practising homosexuality, as well as thieves, greedy, drunkards and worse. 'And such were some of you,' he said to them, 'but you were washed, you were sanctified, you were justified in the name of the Lord Jesus Christ and by the Spirit of our God' (1 Cor. 6:11). Wonderfully, this is just as true of the church today – whatever we once were, we are now washed, sanctified and justified through our Saviour, the Lord Jesus Christ.

Scars from sin

But recovering sinners still bear the scars of the past. So where there is real gospel ministry, where God's Spirit is at work changing lives, there will be real mess unearthed in people's lives. So we must be honest, and very realistic, if we are going to fruitfully help one another in Christ's name. And help *is* always needed in this area; sin is always crouching at the door for all of us (Gen. 4:7). We need to be alert. And we need to build healthy thinking into our whole outlook, so that we will be people who keep to God's path, no matter how dark or difficult or wrong our past has been.

For some of us that past is very complicated and we cannot be naïve about how much harder it can make life subsequently. So as always, prevention is much, much better than cure, and I hope that this chapter will help you not just to think about these issues in your own life, but to encourage and help others also. It will be important for parents in thinking about teaching and training their children, but also for older people, whom Paul says have a responsibility to help younger married people in this area (e.g. 1 Tim. 5, Titus 2), and of course for young Christians whose active hormones need to be harnessed and directed in a good and healthy direction!

MARRIAGE IS FROM GOD

The first thing Jesus does is take us right back to the beginning of human history, to creation itself. 'Have you not read that he who created them from the beginning made them male and female, and said, "Therefore a man shall leave his father and his mother and hold fast to his wife, and they shall become one flesh"?' (Matt. 19:4-5). God is the Giver, the Creator of marriage. He who created humanity created sexuality and commanded the union of the sexes in a permanent public bond of marriage. A man and woman leave their primary families and they are united publicly in a new family unit, and because it is God who gives this gift, man must not undo it (19:6).

The Creator's healthy order

Jesus' point is therefore very clear: marriage is not just a social convention; it is not just a cultural custom. Marriage is not man's invention but God's, and Jesus says this is part of the very order of Creation. This is not just *Christian* marriage; there is no other kind of marriage. This is *human* marriage, ordained at the very dawn of creation. Hence marriage is often called a 'creation ordinance'. It is part of God's universal order for all humanity.

Genesis chapters 1 and 2 clearly speak of the creation of a material order in the universe, but Jesus is saying they speak also of the creation of a foundational moral order. So to reject the moral order God has created is not just sin, it is also folly. If human society is created to work this way, then it must be extremely foolish to seek to subvert it and find another way – every bit as foolish as trying to pretend that gravity is not part of the created order. If you do, and walk off a high roof, you will make a big mess. In just the same way, ignoring and defying God's moral order will inevitably lead to a mess for humanity. We should not be surprised that in the half century and more since the so-called 'sexual revolution' began in our western culture, we have not seen the glorious nirvana of human flourishing and freedom it promised, in terms of more and better sex, and more fulfilling relationships. Indeed, quite the reverse.

Society's unhealthy disorder

The great irony is that there is considerable evidence to indicate that people are having both less sex, and less satisfying sex lives today, than

40

decades ago.[1] And, as we noted in the previous chapter, we are living amid an unprecedented epidemic of loneliness and social fracture. This is just part of the ensuing mess when people exchange God's true order for life and loving for the alluring, but false, promise of autonomy, freedom and self-fulfilment through doing it all your own way. And, as is so often the case, it is the most vulnerable in society who are paying the highest price for our society's disdain for the biblical understanding of marriage.

There is overwhelming evidence to show that children have better outcomes in almost every area of life when they grow up in a home with their two biological parents in a stable marriage. Marriage break-up damages children, and their future. Today's trend for co-habitation rather than marriage is even worse news for the vulnerable young, because such relationships are far less stable than marriage. In the UK today fully two-thirds of all co-habiting parents split up. Such is the decline in marriages that break-ups in co-habiting parents account for 80 percent of all family ruptures. Almost half of all children born in the UK today will no longer be living with both parents by their sixteenth birthday.[2]

Moreover, it is overwhelmingly among lower-income families that marriage is now least prevalent; marriage is increasingly the preserve of the rich. And so, as Glynn Harrison notes, 'After imposing their liberal views on the poorest, the better off are reaping the benefits of marriage for themselves.'[3]

---

1   Spiegelhalter, D. J., *Sex by Numbers: What Statistics Can Tell Us about Sexual Behaviour*, (Profile Books, 2015), p. 30.

2   Harrison, G., *A Better Story: God, Sex & Human Flourishing*, (IVP, 2016), p. 108. I am grateful for Glynn Harrison's extremely helpful and illuminating critique of the societal effects of the sexual revolution in Chapters 8-11 of *A Better Story*, and commend it for further reading.

3   Ibid, p. 109.

Christianity's enlightened message

We can see before our very eyes the effects of all the assaults upon marriage, and the results are far from happy. The war on marriage is, above all, a war on the weak. So we have no reason to be on the back foot in defending marriage as God intended it to be. Indeed, to protect and promote marriage is as much a campaign for social justice and social mobility as it is for moral integrity. 'The promotion of strong marriages and families is potentially one of our most fruitful contributions to the common good.'[4] So, let us not be slow, as Christians, to talk up the goodness of this gift of God. Marriage is God's creation. It is God's gracious gift to all humanity.

A gift of God

But it is therefore a *gift* and as such it is primarily a responsibility that is to be exercised and not a right that is to be demanded. That is important because it explains why it is a natural desire for men and women to want to marry and have family and yet, for any individual in particular, it is not a right to be assumed. This gift may be withheld from some for various reasons, and sometimes those reasons are known only to God.

Jesus is quite plain that not all will marry: 'Not everyone can receive this,' He says, 'for there are eunuchs who have been so from birth, there are eunuchs who have been made eunuchs by men, and there are eunuchs who have made themselves eunuchs for the sake of the kingdom of heaven' (Matt. 19:11-12). Jesus says some people remain celibate for many different reasons, including congenital or acquired physical problems (like eunuchs, who had been castrated), personality issues and so on. Sometimes life experience has made marriage an impossibility, perhaps due to damaging experiences earlier on in life, or perhaps illness or just the passage of time. But Jesus says it might also be for the sake of more fruitfully serving the kingdom of heaven – as was the case for the Lord Himself.

---

4   Ibid, p. 107.

So not all are going to be married according to this Creation pattern. That is very important, because it helps us see that marriage, even as a good gift from God, is not an end in itself. Rather, it is a means to an end. The reason and the purpose for marriage is the same as for every other earthly relationship; it is to serve the kingdom of heaven. This is so vital to grasp, whether you are married or not yet married, whether a confirmed bachelor or spinster, or a single person desperately wanting not to be single. Marriage is a gift and therefore to be received as a gift if God wills, not snatched out of His hand as a right. Moreover, marriage is not just a gift; it is a gift with a purpose.

MARRIAGE IS FOR GOD

Marriage is a gift that God gives to humanity to serve His eternal kingdom. Its purpose mirrors the creation of humanity in the first place: to glorify God. Man's 'chief end', his ultimate purpose, is to glorify God, which means to serve God and His glorious kingdom.[5] So marriage, too, is part of that purpose. God made the different sexes, and marriage between them, to serve His goal in creation and redemption. Therefore every aspect of the marriage relationship must be defined by this relationship to God's eternal kingdom.

A single defining relationship

That is the whole context of Jesus' teaching in Matthew 19: it is a chapter all about what really defines our most important earthly relationships. Is it heaven and God's kingdom, or is it earth and our desires? Does our desire for marriage, or for money (which Jesus deals with in the second half of the chapter) define how we relate to God? Or does our relationship with God and His heavenly kingdom dictate our view of all these earthly gifts?

---

5   Here, and elsewhere throughout this book, I am indebted to Christopher Ash for his *Marriage: Sex in the Service of God* (IVP, 2003), an outstanding work of comprehensive exegesis, theology and ethics which has illuminated my thinking very helpfully in some of the areas we are looking at.

The whole controversy with the Pharisees was because they were *using* God's word to get what *they* wanted: in this case easy divorce and sexual pleasure with another partner. But Jesus points them to marriage's proper meaning in relation to God's purpose and *His* kingdom. He says that marriage, and indeed our whole attitude to marriage or singleness, must be defined in relation to how we serve the kingdom of heaven. That is true whether we are married or celibate. It is all to be for the sake of the kingdom of heaven.

Read through Matthew 19 to see how often Jesus reiterates references to the kingdom of heaven. Repeatedly He speaks of *eternal life*, treasures in *heaven*, and the *new world* (e.g. verses 14, 16, 17, 21, 23, 24, 28, 29). All through the chapter, Jesus says the kingdom of heaven is what must define all our earthly relationships. That is true in marriage, with children ('for of such is the kingdom of heaven' vv. 13-14), and with possessions – the issue for the rich young man (v. 21): treasure in heaven is what matters. Earthly relationships are good *only* if they help, and do not hinder, the kingdom of heaven (vv. 29-30); therefore those who give up relationships which will hinder the kingdom of heaven will be richly blessed and rewarded by the Lord.

The context of this chapter makes it very clear: it is heavenly relationships, and serving Christ's heavenly kingdom, which together must dictate the goal and the purpose of all earthly relationships, and that is true above all in the closest and the most powerful human relationship: sexual union in marriage. It is also true whether you, personally, are married or not. Marriage is from God, it is a gift; but it is also, above all, for God.

A single ultimate purpose

We need to be very clear that marriage is *for* God and for His kingdom purposes, because this is the underlying foundation for the three more commonly considered reasons for marriage included in traditional Christian marriage services. Our marriage service says that marriage is ordained for the continuance of family life and for children; for lifelong mutual help and comfort, in both prosperity and adversity, of one spouse for the other; and, thirdly, for the welfare of human society. The Confession of Faith of our church (and many others) repeats the same truths this way, 'Marriage was ordained for the mutual help of husband and wife; for the increase of mankind with a legitimate issue, and of the church with an holy seed; and for prevention of uncleanness'.[6] But the primary purpose *all* of these serve, through the mutual and complementary partnership of male and female in marriage, is the furtherance of God's purpose in this world, which in turn is all about serving the everlasting kingdom of our Lord Jesus Christ.

The words about marriage Jesus quotes from Genesis remind us that the chief purpose of man's very creation is to glorify God in all things: humanity is to serve as God's glorious image on earth, ruling and having dominion over all creation. Each aspect of marriage, therefore, helps in achieving that God-given role for mankind, to fulfil God's ultimate purpose for this world. In speaking of both the Creation of this world and of the kingdom of heaven, the 'new world', Jesus brings these things together. He shows us we are never to think of marriage without seeing its fundamental purpose: serving His glory in Creation *and* in ultimate New Creation through God's plan of redemption.

To understand Jesus' teaching, it is helpful for us to recall Genesis 1-2, to see how the three 'Ps' of marriage – partnership, procreation and protection – all find their place in this primary understanding of marriage, which was task-driven and goal-oriented towards serving God's kingdom from the very beginning.

Partnership and Procreation in Marriage

Genesis 1:27, where Jesus bases His argument, says, 'God created man in his own image, in the image of God he created him; *male and female* he created them.' But why did He create them male and female?

---

6   Westminister Confession of Faith, 24:2.

Fruitfully filling the earth

The answer, of course, lies in the immediate context: 'Let us make man in our image, after our likeness. And let them have dominion...' over all that is in the earth (Gen. 1:26). Humans are to image God in order to rule, under Him, the whole of creation. So the task of dominion is the context for God's differentiation of mankind as male and female. Likewise, in this context is the command to *procreate*: 'Be fruitful and multiply and fill the earth, subdue it, and have dominion....' (v. 28).

God brings human beings into a world full of life and potential which needs ruling, and that unique task is given to man. And since that task can only be fulfilled through procreation, this is the context of man's creation as a sexual being (male and female) and as a procreative being. They must fill the earth in order to bring God's gracious rule to its outermost parts, and to do this, procreation is required, and ordained, by God.[7] So the focus of sexual differentiation in Genesis 1 is this *procreative* purpose of marriage, the first of those 'Ps', in order that man can serve God's purpose for mankind and have dominion over His kingdom.

Then Genesis 2 gives a second account of man's creation as a sexually differentiated being. This is not a rival or contradictory account of Creation; Genesis 1 simply describes Creation from the point of view of its cosmic purpose, while Chapter 2 describes it with a particular human focus: we move from man as the crown of Creation to man as the centre of Creation.

Mutually serving the earth

Jesus also quotes Genesis 2:24, which rounds off the story of Eve's creation from Adam. Christopher Ash helpfully points out the mistake commonly made by lifting verse 18 right out of context: 'It is not good

---

7   'On the one hand, towards the Creator, humankind is given moral responsibility; on the other, towards Creation, he is entrusted with a task, and the coordination of both these aspects of this orientation is the key to the ethics of sex'. Ash, Christopher, *Marriage: Sex in the Service of God* (IVP, 2003), p. 103.

that man should be alone.' We often assume that 'alone' there means *lonely*, so we think that the primary purpose of marriage is a cure for loneliness. But though the comfort and companionship marriage brings are very important, that is not the primary focus here. We have already seen that all the way through the Bible the primary solution for loneliness is not marriage and sex, but friendship and fellowship. Intimacy and belonging do *not* require a sexual relationship, whatever our sex-obsessed world thinks, and shouts so loudly. No. Sexual relationships were not created because man was lonely, and needed *sex*, but because he was lacking something needed for *service* – to God and His Creation.

Genesis 2:18 is very plain. Adam's situation is not good because he needs a *helper*; but the question is, what does he need a helper for? The answer is that he needs a helper for the task of working God's creation, to properly fulfil God's purpose for it. In Genesis 2:5 we are told there was no order on the earth, because as yet 'there was no man to work the ground.' So God forms man to meet this need in creation, and bring it to completion (2:7). 'The Lord God took the man and put him in the garden of Eden *to work it and keep it*' (2:15). In other words, the task described in Genesis 1:28 as having dominion and subduing creation is called here working and keeping the garden. We are meant to see man's task on earth as being to extend the beauty and the order of God's garden of Eden right out into the whole of the created cosmos. Man, as God's image, is to take God's perfect pattern and to bring it to the whole of His creation.

But it is for this task that Adam is as yet incomplete. He needs help. He needs just the right sort of helper, a helper 'fit for him' (2:18), meaning not just one of the myriad of earthly creatures God has made, but a suitably complementary *human* helper – a partner in serving God's purpose for Creation. This is the primary purpose of the *partnership* aspect of marriage. It is a partnership to serve the purpose of God's kingdom in the world. The mutuality of sexual love within marriage is not the *goal* of marriage, it is there to *serve* the true goal, which is bringing God's kingdom into its glorious fulness.

What Genesis 1-2 teaches about the foundation of human marriage is so important because it helps us see that both *procreation* within marriage and the personal *partnership* of mutual help in marriage are given to serve the primary calling of all mankind, which is glorifying God through serving His glorious purpose for the world. It is this understanding of marriage that Jesus Himself so clearly affirms.

Marriage's continuing purpose

Of course, all of this in Genesis 1 and 2 is before the rebellion of man – the Fall,[8] before sin wrecks God's creation. Yet the rest of Genesis teaches that the primary purpose for marriage persists for humans – although now the world's urgent need is for rescue. The Creation goal of dominion over God's world by man can only ever come about now through God's plan of redemption.

Just filling the world with people – sinful people – can't be the answer to this world, can it? Humanity's sinful state now naturally only reproduces people in sin – the seed of the Serpent (Gen. 3:15). But God's promise brings a new start, through the procreation of a new family, not just multiplying people but multiplying the seed of God, the seed of promise. From Genesis 12 onwards, the unfolding story of God's blessing of human procreation begins to focus especially on Abraham and his offspring, the people of Israel. They are to be the beginning of God's new humanity, a people chosen and called out to serve God's plan of redemption through which the whole world will at last be recreated to fulfil its ultimate purpose. And it was indeed marriage and procreation, through the seed of the woman, the offspring of Abraham, which brought about ultimate redemption at last through a new and true Adam, the Lord Jesus Christ.

---

8   'The Fall' is not a particularly helpful term. There was nothing remotely accidental about man's primal rebellion against God, which the Bible describes clearly as Adam's 'transgression', 'trespass' & 'disobedience' (Rom. 5:14, 15, 19).

Nevertheless, the story of this world is not yet complete. So, until Jesus comes again to finally end this present age and usher in His eternal kingdom, human marriage still has this same task: to serve God's ultimate purpose for creation. And since as believers in Christ we know that the goal of creation can only be fulfilled through redemption in Christ, it must be clear that for us to serve God's creation purpose today through marriage means that the primary purpose of our marriages must be to serve the kingdom of Christ and its advance in this world. We will do that through procreation; but not that alone. Filling the world with godly offspring is certainly one way to grow the church. But they must also be *missionary* children because that is what we are all called for. God's 'offspring' today are being gathered in to join His kingdom family from every tribe and every nation through the spreading of the gospel of Christ. And so our Christian marriages, and our Christian homes, exist to serve that missionary task – not least by nurturing heralds of the kingdom for the next generation.

If you are a Christian parent raising children, that may very well be one of your most important – even your primary – roles in life: serving the kingdom of God and advancing His kingdom by raising children, teaching and training them in the ways of the gospel of Christ, and encouraging them to be missionary ambassadors for the Lord Jesus. So if you are a harassed mother, just about demented by young kids who are driving you crazy, and you think you can't cope with another day, don't despair! You need to know yours is a great calling; and the Lord God will help you, if you ask Him, to raise heralds of the gospel of Christ. As churches, too, that should be our prayer for all our young ones, for those that we are teaching and training – because all procreation and family life is *for* the service of the kingdom of Christ. Likewise, the way we think of the relationship of mutual sexual partnership in marriage must be focused on serving the kingdom of God. The 'face-to-face', romantic, erotic love of marriage is there *for* the 'side-by-side' task of kingdom service (Phil. 1:27).

Missionary marriages?

It is worth pausing to ponder whether we really think this way about marriage and family life. It is so foreign to the world around us, which tells us that relationship and sex is for us, to serve us, and that children are for us, if and when we want them. The world's thinking so easily shapes our attitudes in this whole area.

It is easy just to perpetuate unconsciously the idea that marriage is all about satisfaction for us, rather than service for God. So Christian marriages run into trouble, just like others, because of dissatisfaction and disappointment within the relationship. The 'face to face' becomes an end in itself, not the enabling and enriching means of strengthening the 'side by side' task of serving Christ in the world. Too often the answer to disappointment is simply dissolution.

Likewise, Christians often have goals and ambitions for their children which have much more to do with success in our culture than service of the kingdom. This elevation of the ephemeral over the eternal means that churches, too, are often under great pressure from parents not to make their youth work 'too heavy' on things like Bible teaching, lest their youngsters are put off Christian things.

If you are tempted to think that way, you need to know it is the sure-fire way of preventing youngsters from gaining the resolute Christian character which alone will protect them from the world's alluring voices. You also need to ask yourself if you have really understood God's purpose of procreation within marriage, and above all within Christian marriages. If marriage is truly to be held in honour among all, we need to think deeply about how the gift of partnership and procreation in marriage finds its real fulfilment in fruitful service of His kingdom.

Protection of marriage

It was of course the spoiling of sin after the Fall which made a necessity of the third 'P' of the marriage purpose, *protection*. The sanctity of the marriage bond is a protection for the community and society as a whole: protecting sexual decency, safeguarding the integrity of the family unit, sheltering children, and acting as a public preventative to the damaging consequences of sin where sexual activity is not kept within God's permitted boundaries, and thus is detrimental to true human flourishing. That is why the marriage service says that society can prosper only when the marriage bond is held in the highest honour. This reflects the Bible's consistent emphasis, instructing us very clearly that the only right and proper place for sexual relations is within monogamous, faithful marriage.

God's word warns us of the dangers of ignoring this, and protects marital fidelity with serious sanctions for violation of God's instruction. The Old Testament law prescribed severe penalities for marriage violation (e.g. Deut. 22:13-30; Lev. 18), and though the penalities may differ in the New Testament era, the same sanctions clearly apply. Jesus Himself strengthens the commands about marital fidelity, and Paul echoes these Old Testament passages to call the Corinthians to 'purge the evil' of sexual immorality from the church (1 Cor. 5:1-13).

Because it is such an important protector *of* society, the institution of marriage needs to be protected within society, and *for* society. When it is not, and when the exclusive dignity of real marriage is eroded in law, as is increasingly happening in our post-Christian, secular culture (as well as in parts of the professing Christian church), then the Bible warns us: there will be damage to family life, community life and to society as a whole.

Biblical realism is desperately needed

The problem for our society is that secularist politicians are very slow to understand this. For one thing, they have little, if any, place for a concept of human sin, and it is very difficult to govern sinful people wisely if you neither understand sin, nor the truth about the real source of evil in this world. The Bible is much more realistic than our politicians; it will not try to place all the problems we face in life as coming from 'somewhere out there', so that if only 'society' was truly liberated and free, all our individual problems would fade away and vanish. Jesus tells us the very opposite is true: it is 'from within, from the heart of man' that comes all the evil which corrupts and blights human society, not least sexual immorality and adultery (Mark 7:20-23).

Marriage – where it flourishes as God intends, as an exclusive, lifelong union of one man and one woman – protects society from so much that is not only displeasing to Him, but damaging to us also. So if we love and care for our society, we should be deeply concerned about the damage done to marriage as an institution in recent times. We must seek to promote and demonstrate strong and healthy marriage and family life in every way we can, both to please God, and to bless the world.

Marriage for the Christian and the Church

Understanding the purpose of marriage will change the way that we think about marriage – whether we're in it or not, wanting it, or indeed content not to have it for ourselves – because Jesus says that whatever state we are in, it is to be *for* the kingdom of heaven.

It is striking that the New Testament has comparatively little to say in detail about our relationships, but so much about God's redemption. I wonder if thinking about our own lives reflects that same emphasis? We expend an awful lot of thought about marriage and sex, our needs, our feelings, our desires for companionship, perhaps our desires for children and so on. But how much thought do we give to these things within an understanding of the great task marriage exists to serve: God's rescue of a lost world? If we understand that purpose, that the reason for marriage is primarily for serving the kingdom of God, then that must affect our thinking about every aspect of marriage, whether we are married personally or not .

Seeking partnership for service

First, it will affect our thinking about the *partnership* side of marriage: that will be transformed, because it is no longer primarily about meeting our needs for intimacy or preventing loneliness, it is for partnership in better serving the kingdom of Christ.

That means, for one thing, that the answer to those who are lonely and miserable is not to pin all your hopes on a sexual relationship and upon marriage. That is not what marriage is for. So if that is where you are looking for fulfilment of all your life's desires, you will likely only find real disappointment. That is one of the reasons why many marriages today fail, even Christian ones: people are looking to marriage to give them something that marriage was never designed to give. If God's gift to you is marriage, it is not for your salvation, but for your better service. So don't seek salvation in marriage. Seek the service of God's kingdom, and if marriage will truly help *you* in service of the kingdom, God will give you that. You can trust Him.

But at the same time, the church is the family of God, and since this is the way God brings the lonely into families, to answer people's real needs, then 'family' is what should mark us out. Churches should be places where people belong, and therefore one big purpose of marriage, for those who are married and who do have families, is to open their families towards others. If a marriage and a home is closed, and closed-in on itself, then it is unlikely to be serving its purpose for the kingdom, and drawing others in. Neither the married nor the single should be lonely in the family of Christ. That is a big challenge for all of us. It means that the married must not be self-preoccupied, taken up with their own relationships in a way that excludes others, and it means that the single mustn't be self-pitying, because that attitude can make it much harder for others to include them and to help them be part of a family that belongs.

Rightly understanding the purpose of the marriage partnership also means that the church's focus, for example in marriage preparation or in counselling, will be right. It cannot be focused merely on the personal relationship and the sexual side of marriage. Virtually all secular marriage courses, and even many Christian ones, are thoroughly introspective, focused chiefly on developing intimacy and a better relationship. Those things are helpful up to a point, but the church's task is to take us beyond that need-centred and me-focused approach, to teach that marriage is task-focused, and that we are to prepare people for serving God's kingdom in the world. So our whole attitude to the personal side of marriage will be transformed when we see the Bible's focus on marriage's true purpose and reason.

Transforming our parenthood

Secondly, our whole attitude to *procreation* in marriage will likewise be transformed; it can never be just about our wanting babies and wanting families, natural as that is (or indeed, of not wanting them). We will not be paedo-centric, totally child-focused and obsessed, as our culture has increasingly become – obsessed with children, obsessed with their achievements, obsessed with all sorts of things to the extent we virtually worship our children. As we will see in Chapter Seven, our focus as Christians, and in the church, will be child rearing for God's kingdom purposes: nurturing our own children at home, and concerned with the nurture of all children in the church, to be Kingdom builders for the Lord Jesus Christ. That is our task because that is marriage's purpose.

Enlarging our horizons

And of course, our understanding of the place of marriage for *protecting* and preserving society will be very clear as well; we will understand that marriage is not just a private relationship, but a public one, affecting others and not just ourselves. Marriage is a gift of God for the service of His purposes of grace: both His *common grace* to all humanity, in blessing this whole world with order and not chaos, and with an abundance of good gifts for human life, but also His *saving grace* through serving the mission of the church. Knowing this must affect how we think as Christians about marriage when we face significant struggles in our own marriages, and very especially should we find ourselves starting to think about separation and about divorce. My marriage is not just about me and my personal happiness; it is not even just about my children's welfare. No, my marriage is about something much, much bigger. It is about God's purpose for creation and redemption; it is about the preservation of society; and it is certainly about the health and the witness of the church in society.

So you can see how understanding marriage's reason and purpose in Scripture transforms the way we ought to think about all these things.

Remembering Jesus

But, finally: these things are, of course, deeply personal, and I realise that for some of us this whole area may be deeply painful. Thinking about these things might lift the lid on a great deal of pain, maybe even a great deal of sin in the past, or even in the present. And so the final thing I want to say is this: just two words – *remember Jesus*!

Jesus will not hide the truth from you, nor will He let you hide from the truth, however painful that may be; there is no cheap grace with the Lord Jesus Christ. He puts His finger right on the painful sore that is making us very uncomfortable. Think of the woman at the well; He put His finger right on the issue in her life, 'You have had five husbands and the man you are with now is not even your husband.' But when He does do that, He does it only ever to bring healing, to draw you, like that woman, to the life-giving cleansing of His living water. 'Come to me,' He said to all such; 'all who labour and are heavy laden, come to me and I will give you rest.' And He still says that today. So, if you find yourself feeling that kind of deep pain in this whole area of the heart: remember Jesus.

3. The Road to Marriage

Once we have understood God's purpose for sexual relationships, we can ask how we go about finding our way into marriage – if that is to be God's gift for us. We need to understand the purpose of sex before we think about the pathway to marriage, because unless we know what something is *for*, we are very likely to misuse it, make a mess and get badly hurt.

As we have seen, the Bible affirms only one kind of sexual relationship, marriage between one man and one woman, and so the terms 'sexual relationship' and 'marriage' are interchangeable. Indeed marriage is defined by sex: the married bond is consummated by sexual intimacy (hence the rupture caused by adultery).[1] Marriage is for sex, just as sex is for marriage.

Just because something *can* be used for a particular purpose, it does not mean it is meant for that purpose. Think about petrol. Petrol is for running a car; petrol is not for starting your barbecue! I learned this some years ago, not from a book, but in my garden. My barbecue would not start so, having a petrol can in my garage, I thought I would improvise. I was very careful. I didn't just pour it on, I carefully

---

1   This is just one reason why what our governments now call 'same-sex marriage' is not real marriage at all. In the UK, the law gives what it calls same-sex 'marriage' no definition of consummation, nor of breach by adultery, thus it cannot be marriage by any historic understanding of the term.

soaked some newspaper and put it gingerly on the barbecue, and very cautiously lit a match at arm's length. But there was a very big bang, and I lost my eyebrows – and the respect of my wife! Well, sex is equally explosive, equally dangerous. Just because sex can be used for certain purposes does not mean that is what it is really for. It does not mean it is not dangerous if we use it the wrong way.

What sex is *for*, as we have discovered, is the service of God. Marriage was given to serve God's kingdom. The three particular blessings of marriage, the three 'Ps' of marriage, all serve that primary goal: Partnership, the mutual sexual union of marriage; Procreation, child bearing, nurturing and training; and Protection through the public recognition of marriage to prevent wrongful and damaging sexual relationships taking place outside marriage. This last 'P', of course, is necessary since the Fall of man because sin so easily corrupts that primary purpose of marriage. So the reason for marriage is to serve the kingdom of God by these means.

But how do we find a good marriage partner, and start in a way that builds a good marriage from the beginning? What is the healthy road to marriage?

Navigating the path

Obviously this question is especially important for young people, but not only for them. The New Testament commands all of us to honour marriage; it is a public thing and so, in the Christian church especially, we all have a responsibility to help one another to honour God in marriage whether we ourselves are married or not, or ever will be. That is reason enough to take it very seriously. But of course there are a lot of practical reasons. Those of us who are parents need wisdom for our children's relationships as they develop; fathers who have daughters growing up, in particular, can get a bit edgy about these things (I speak from experience!). We also all have a responsibility to support friends in the developing relationships they may find themselves in.

We are all our brother and sister's keepers, but failure to help guard and keep them in this area, through reluctance to get involved in awkward and difficult conversations, is a common failing. So much damaging relational fallout would be prevented were there more serious support from faithful Christian friends. And even confirmed bachelors and spinsters can get a surprise from time to time: I have conducted weddings in the last few years with brides ranging all the way from the second decade to the seventh, so even if you think the road to marriage is unlikely to be your particular journey, you never know!

The problem is that navigating this path to marriage has often proved difficult for many. The key reason for this, I think, is that we in the church have imbibed so much of our culture's corrupted thinking that we so easily miss the true purpose of sexual relationship. Indeed, nearly all our problems about marriage and sexual relationships stem from this; problems in practice always stem from problems in thinking, problems of theology. So we need to think about how the rightful place of the sexual relationship has been reversed in our society – and how we as the church must reclaim it.

THE WORLD HAS REVERSED GOD'S PLACE FOR SEX

Our world has reversed the proper place and purpose of the sexual relationship. This is utterly plain in our twenty-first century western culture; we live in a society that no longer recognises that the sexual relationship of marriage is for God – it thinks the opposite. Our society worships the sexual relationship *as* God.

Of course, this is something humans have always done, as the Bible shows. The pagan Canaanite idols which lured ancient Israelites away from the Lord in Old Testament times were nearly all sex and fertility gods and goddesses. Their flamboyant worship involved ritual temple prostitution and sexual orgies; hence the great allure of such religion, especially to men. The Greco-Roman culture of the New

Testament was equally replete with sexual licence, lavish eroticism, and widespread homosexuality. People often fail to realise this, and think that the Bible writers are naïve and ignorant of sexual things. The reality is the opposite. They lived surrounded by unbridled sexuality, and all its consequences. So, they do not speak to us out of Victorian prudery. Their trenchant critique comes from deep experience, and so is as relevant to us today as to the first readers.

But the (essentially pagan) deification of sex is something that has again become greatly magnified in our Western society in the last few generations, as we have jettisoned the Christian heritage we once cherished, and which had influenced our culture so significantly in this area, as in all others. Our morality, as with our laws and institutions, all stood on firm Christian foundations. That is no longer true as we have steadily de-Christianised, and we are now more like the First Century culture of the New Testament than perhaps at any time since the Emperor Constantine Christianised the Roman Empire in the Fourth Century AD.

Sex as god

Here is how the Apostle Paul, in that First Century, described the human condition without Christ: 'For although they knew God, they did not honour him as God or give thanks to him, but they became futile in their thinking, and their foolish hearts were darkened' (Rom. 1:21). This, too, is what we see writ large all around us today: as a society we do not honour God, our thinking is futile, our hearts are far from Him. And the result of this, says Paul, is sexual idolatry: 'Therefore God gave them up in the lusts of their hearts to impurity, to the dishonouring of their bodies among themselves, *because* they exchanged the truth about God for a lie and worshipped and served the creature rather than the Creator' (Rom. 1:24–25). The characteristic that sums up a sexually confused and a sexually promiscuous and obsessed society is idolatry. If people stop worshipping the Creator and start worshipping the relationships that they have with one another, especially sinful sexual relationships, sex is no longer *for* God. It *is* God.

Wrong thinking about sexual relationships is perhaps the clearest expression of the basic sin of man, worshipping created things instead of the Creator. That rebellious anti-worship displaces God from the centre of His world so that we become the centre of the universe, and God is banished to the periphery; He becomes our servant instead of the other way round. The rebellious force at the heart of fallen humanity is this relentless tendency to reverse everything in the created order. 'God made man upright but they have sought out many schemes' (Eccles. 7:29). We scheme to reverse the created order in every possible area of life, because we are idolatrous beings, we are rebels deep in our hearts. And the greater the gift of God, the nearer a blessing is to God Himself, the greater the danger of that idolatrous reversal.

This is what we have done with marriage and sex all through the history of humanity, and very aggressively in the last few decades. It is why controversies about sexuality in the mainline churches, about homosexual relationships in particular, are not just about the seventh commandment. They are about the first commandment, about who are we bowing down to. Are we bowing down to The Lord as God? Or to sexual expression, the way we want it, as God?

We need to be clear how pervasive this reversal really is in society and so we must understand the shift in our thinking about sex, and the way that has crept into the church.

The shift in society's thinking

Until at least the early post-war years in the latter part of the twentieth century, marriage was still viewed generally as a public good. It was part and parcel of a healthy society and fitted within a web of family and social relationships. It was clearly bound up with an understanding of child rearing within the commitment of a permanent relationship. Of course there have always been bad marriages, abusive marriages, and broken marriages, but marriage as an institution was still regarded as the bedrock of stable and healthy society. No doubt most people did not think consciously about their marriage serving God's kingdom. But they certainly did see their marriage as much, much more than just a one-to-one relationship of love. It was a public thing, not just private; it was part of the cohesion of community life and society.

That has changed drastically, hasn't it? The 1960s marked the biggest shift, the so-called 'decade of free love'. Of course, the contraceptive pill was the great agent of sexual liberation along with the 'Women's Lib' movement, what we now call feminism. Now, more than fifty years on, today all the focus on sexual relationship is on the relationship and the sex: what it offers, the fulfilment it gives and so on. Procreation is certainly no longer a defining feature of sexual relationship. Nor is the public good of marriage as part of a stable interdependency of family, community and society. Sexual relationships in our world have become supremely private, supremely personal. It is nobody's business but mine. We see that so often in the public-private divide people talk about: what public figures do in private is entirely up to them, it is nothing to do with anybody else. The idea that an MP can be cheating and adulterous privately, but honest and trustworthy in everything public is ludicrous of course, but that is how we seem to think today.

Doing it my way

So not only is God left out of the business of sex and marriage, but everybody else is left out too. It is not the business of family or the community; it is not the business of society to interfere. It is a private matter, *my* business. Everything is about *us* and our relationships. But of course, at heart, our focus is even narrower than that. We are actually very self-centred and the sexual relationship has all become about *self*-fulfilment. Our relationships, if we are honest, are not really just about us, but about *me*. It is all about *my* needs, *my* fulfilment, *my* sense of worth; it is about *my* sense of identity, letting me be *me*. It is about doing things *my* way.

This is Romans 1:25 writ large. We are worshipping the created thing, the sexual relationship, rather than the Creator who gave the gift to bless us as we use it to serve Him *His* way. And when we live like that, we are rebellious idolaters, bowing down to sexual relationships. We think that they are able to give us all the things that we need, all the things that we want in life, as though sex were somehow our saviour. 'When all of this has happened to sex', as Christopher Ash says, 'there is no alternative but to deify it. Sex as a source of fulfilment is sex as saviour.'[2]

That is what the commentator Malcolm Muggeridge so famously captured when he said, 'Sex is the substitute religion of the 20th century...the orgasm has replaced the Cross as the focus of longing and fulfilment.'[3] In another place he says, 'If God is dead, somebody is going to have to take his place. It will be megalomania or erotomania, the drive for power or the drive for pleasure, the clenched fist or the phallus, Hitler or Hugh Hefner [head of the *Playboy* empire].'[4] To see that this is how our society today thinks about sex and sexual relationships we only need to think of all the books, TV programmes, articles and videos aiming to improve your sex-life which abound today. Now, do not misunderstand; there is a place for good advice about sex. Sex does come naturally to people, but good sex does not, and the Bible definitely wants good and godly sexual relationships in marriage. The apostle Paul makes that clear in 1 Corinthians 7, and the Song of Songs celebrates godly, erotic love. So there is a place for teaching and helping people with these things, especially newly-weds. The church should not be prudish about these things. The Bible is very down to earth, even earthy in some places.

---

2   Ash, Christopher, *Marriage: Sex in the Service of God* (IVP, 2003), p. 52.

3   Muggeridge, Malcolm, http://libraryofquotes.com/quote/873968 Last accessed 13 December 2018.

4   Muggeridge, Malcolm, *A Third Testament* (Ballantine Books, 1983).

Sex as Saviour

But instead of that, our society has made sex into our saviour. Bookshops are full of books that deify sex, even talking about its mystical, religious aspects. The agony columns even in broadsheet newspapers are dominated by sexual issues. Most of all, the pornography industry is the ultimate worship leader of the great god sex. Even liberal commentators are now noting with some alarm that the effect of this on marriages, on relationships in general, and especially on young people and children, is terribly damaging. People's expectations have been so manipulated, so heightened, so twisted by the world of cyber-sex that, to many, real sex has become dissatisfying and disappointing and drab. A huge number of marriage-related problems, probably the majority today, are sex-related; that is certainly my experience as a pastor, and most pastors will say the same. The sexual relationship is no longer delivering what people expect it to deliver.

But if sex (and marriage itself) is your god, then you are in for disappointment, because it is a dumb idol. It is a created thing, it is not your Creator, and it cannot save you. No human relationship can deliver what people are expecting a sexual relationship to deliver today, not even a good marriage. And that is why it is no surprise that in a society that thinks sex is saviour, our relationship breakup rate is so high. While the absolute number of divorces has declined in the UK in recent years, still around 42 percent of marriages will end in divorce, around half in the first ten years of marriage, with the median marriage lasting twelve years.[5] But as we have noted, far fewer marriages are happening, and the alternative, cohabiting couples, have a far higher break-up rate. Think of the vast trail of disappointment, hurt and bitterness that comes from this. People do have a sense that the 'sex god' does not always deliver salvation. That is why there is a great reluctance to commit, in case it does all go wrong. So what rules now in our society is serial monogamy: sex but no commitment, not till much,

---

5   Rainscourt Family Law Solicitors, https://www.rainscourt.com/interesting-statistics/ Last accessed 19 July 2018.

much later when at last somehow you can be sure that this is the one, that this is your 'soul mate'. And yet the evidence is that people who cohabit in that way massively increase their risk of marriage breakup when marriage does finally come.[6] But ours is a society of commitment later, marriage later, children later (if at all), after all those things you want to have and you want to do, those things you want to do for *you*. And the tragedy is that when many leave it so late like that, they find that the things they *do* want, like a family, are not nearly so easy to come by as they thought. We find that our human creative power is both limited, and time-limited.

All this is the tragedy of a world that has reversed sex's place in life – taken the gift of God, and worshipped it *as* god. It is a god which, like all idols, can deliver nothing and yet, like all idols, is very powerful to deceive and to rob and to destroy. So the sex industry is the world's oldest, and biggest industry. And it is an industry of cynical manipulators bringing huge misery for those who are being exploited.

Society's seepage into the Church

The truth is that the shift in society has inevitably seeped into the Church. Sometimes this is in stark ways, but more often it is subtle. Many Christians seem to make marriage itself their primary goal in life. It is easy for us to see the path to real fulfilment, to real significance and satisfaction, as being in that dream relationship we are desperate to have. And so for many Christians, this becomes an all-consuming thought. It can dominate your prayer life if you are single; that can make it sound very spiritual, but what you really want is for God to serve your desire for a relationship, not the other way around. It also can be true if you are married, if your marriage and your family become your idol. Then you start to think that the church is there, and God is there, and everybody else is there, to serve you and your desires *your* way, not the other way around. We are greatly influenced by our

---

6   See Harrison, G., *A Better Story: God, Sex & Human Flourishing*, (IVP, 2016), p108.

consumerist, self-focused society, much more affected by it than we realise.

Many, especially young Christians, are full of angst about guidance for this area. They are desperate to know who 'the right person for *me*' is; 'what is God's will for *my* relationship?' Yet, you know, the New Testament is virtually uninterested in such things. What it is interested in, in terms of determining God's will, is telling you to be holy and right and to serve God and His kingdom. '*This is the will of God*,' says Paul to the Thessalonians, 'your sanctification.' (1 Thess. 4:3). 'Rejoice always, pray without ceasing, give thanks in all circumstances, for *this is the will of God in Christ Jesus for you*' (1 Thess. 5:16-18). If you want to know what God's will for your life is, that is what it is!

If all your focus on 'guidance' is on finding that relationship, and you ask, 'What is God's will for me?' then if a Christian leader says *to* you 'God's real will for you is simply that you live a holy, prayerful and thankful life whatever your circumstances', you will probably be impatient, and even cross! But that is because we too, even in the church, have so often reversed the place of marriage and the sexual relationship. We too have been guilty of making it into a god and not a means of serving God. Jesus says we are to seek first the kingdom of God and His righteousness, and if we do then all we need will be added to us (Matt. 6:33) – but in our hearts we say, '*I* know what I need, Lord, so give that to me and *then* I'll seek and serve your kingdom.' Isn't that the case? We want God to bow down and serve our relationships, instead of our relationships to bow down and serve God.

The world's thinking has seeped into our consciousness. We cannot help it; we breathe the air of the world we live in. So we see Christians, too, wanting to wait and wait and wait before committing to marriage. We see Christians cycling through partners, anxiously waiting for the perfect one, and marrying later and later and later. Some are so unwilling to commit that, ultimately, they just miss the boat. In some ways, many Christians are in a worse position than secular people because, as well as the worldly fear of commitment, and the sense they must be sure to find that one elusive 'soul mate', they have a foolish, unbiblical view of guidance. Instead of applying the Bible's rich wisdom to all of life, so as to be truly 'guided' by God's clear teaching, which is what will help us to be holy, prayerful and thankful in *all* things, they expect God to reveal 'His will' to them decisively for every personal circumstance, without which they are unable to make a commitment about anything. Well, if you think like that, especially in the world that we live in, it can only lead to fear and paralysis on the road to marriage.

We must recognise all such wrong and worldly thinking, and we must resist it.

THE CHURCH MUST RECLAIM GOD'S PLACE FOR SEX

Paul says in Colossians 2:6-7, 'As you received Christ Jesus the Lord, so walk in him, rooted and built up in him and established in the faith, just as you were taught, abounding in thanksgiving'. And he goes on, 'See to it that no one takes you captive by philosophy and vain deceit' (Col. 2:8). That is a passionate plea for Christian believers to have clear heads, and for their foundation in all thinking about life to be Christ and His gospel and His kingdom. Nowhere is this more important today than in the area of sex. The church must reclaim the true place, and the true purpose, of the sexual relationship, and therefore reclaim a true and a wise path to marriage.

So let me apply some of the Bible's wisdom and instruction very practically to this area of life because it is this, not the world's folly, which must inform both our thinking and our behaviour on the road to marriage, just as it does in every other area of life. Here are three Do's and three Don't's to help think about this personally if we are going to reclaim a right and healthy road to marriage.

Be Trusting

First, do trust God and His revealed purpose for marriage, and trust the Lord Jesus with your personal life. Put simply, that means get on with serving God's kingdom with all your might and leaving the rest to God. It was as Adam lived out his Creation purpose that God gave him the helper that he needed. Your job too, the purpose of your creation, is to serve Him, to serve His kingdom. And if to fulfil the calling from God for your life you need a helper from God, a marriage partner, God will arrange it. The Sovereign Lord will provide that helper for you, you can trust Him. Seek first His kingdom, and all these things that He knows you need will be added to you. That does not necessarily mean, of course, all the things you *want* – but if we believe Jesus and trust Him, it does mean all the things we need.

So if marriage is for serving God's garden, then put your boots on, get to work in the garden and God will see to the helper that you need! Read Jesus' words in Matthew 6: 'do not be anxious about your life' is the refrain; your Heavenly Father knows what you need, trust Him! And since the purpose of marriage is serving His kingdom, then it makes sense that the more you are engaged in serving Him, the clearer it will become to you and to others the kind of helper you need, if you need one. And, if you do, it will be much easier to find a partner who is also engaged in seeking to serve Christ in that same way. The best Christian marriages so often come when two people are drawn together in love through serving Christ together.

Be Real

Second thing: do be real. A marriage partner, according to the Bible, is to be first of all a helper for your service of God's kingdom, not a hinderer. There is no middle way. A spouse will either help or hinder your spiritual life, and you must be real about that. Many a bloke has been led down a perilous path by a pretty face and flattering eyes, and many a girl by a dazzling guy, to the regret, and sometimes ruin, of both. Don't fool yourself. That is why Paul is plain as a pikestaff in 2 Corinthians 6:14 when he says, 'Do not be unequally yoked with unbelievers.' He is speaking there about every sphere of life but it is especially important in the romantic sphere.

It is utterly basic to a scriptural view of marriage that believers are to marry 'in the Lord' (1 Cor. 7:39) lest marriage be a hindrance; yet it is astonishing how often people deceive themselves and say, 'Well, it'll be different for me.' Is God lying? It will not be different for you! Be real. A partner in marriage, which exists for serving the kingdom of God, must be a fellow worker who will help your service. Do not be hitched to a sluggard, says Proverbs, or a fool, even if they do profess their faith and tell you it is alright now because they are a Christian. Do not choose someone who hinders your service, or may even hinder your salvation.

Remember, too, that in Genesis chapter 2 the woman is not just a helper. We are told she was a suitable helper, she was a good fit. This is primarily speaking about the complementary nature of the sexes, that man and woman are not the same but complement one another. That is God's design (which is why same-sex sexual relationships are such a defiance of the created order). But it is also true on an individual level. Let me state the obvious: partners (in marriage, as in any partnership in life) must be compatible. Of course a little incompatibility *can* be the spice of life! Opposites do often attract; one spouse is often an early bird and the other a night owl, or one is always late and the other always early, and so on. It is sometimes astonishing how people manage to cope with each other!

But be real. If you are determined to spend your whole life in pioneer mission on the frontier deserts of North Africa and the person that you are interested in would never ever consider leaving their home town, you need to be sensible. You need to think about it before you get entangled in a situation that is going to cause heartbreak. Do not let yourself fall crazily in love with someone who will never be a helper in your service to Christ.

Do not be carried away by the kind of romanticism which can so easily obscure harsh reality. Do not think, 'just because I am "in love", it changes everything'. Love *does not* change everything. Lots of married people 'fall in love' with someone other than their spouses – it happens all the time at work and in other places – and it robs them of their rationality. It is just an emotion, it is foolish and frivolous – and wrong. 'Falling in love' can make you stupid. So you need to listen to other people whose heads are screwed on, and not up in the clouds of love like yours. Listen to your friends, especially Christian friends. Listen to your parents; they are not as stupid as you think they are! The book of Proverbs urges young people to listen to both their father's and mother's wisdom, and most fathers can sniff out when Prince Charming is just a bad egg, especially if he is interested in his daughter, just as mothers will be pretty astute about the character of a girl who is turning the head of her son.

The whole business of asking a father's permission to get married is not just a quaint tradition; it speaks of the fact that marriage is a public thing, that it affects everybody, especially your family, and that they have a stake in it. There are many jokes about in-laws, and of course in most marriages there are tensions of various kinds in wider family relationships; that is almost inevitable, simply because a marriage brings together family cultures and traditions that differ. There are always challenges.

But some of us will know of marriages where in-law relations are almost non-existent, or bitterly hostile, because one spouse cannot, or (more often) will not, relate to the other's family. So the creation of a marriage brings destruction to other family relationships. Sometimes the fault lies with parents, but not always, and you must be real about thinking through the consequences carefully before you end up in a marriage which leaves you bereaved of relationship with your own family.

Your family have a stake in your marriage. Your friends have a stake in it, and the church has a stake in it too. Often they can see what you cannot see through your misty eyes, that there is a glaring incompatibility or unsuitability or a great risk. Real friends will help you see it, and be realistic.

Be wise

Thirdly, do be wise: be wise about when it is the time to be seriously on the road to the commitment of marriage. Jesus echoes Genesis and talks about a man and a wife, not a boy and a girl. What He means is that there is a certain maturity involved, a readiness to make a serious commitment in life and *for* life. This is a new 'cleaving' (Gen. 2:24 KJV) which comes with a new stage in life, leaving immaturity and adolescence behind.

Of course, many factors influence what that age is for any particular person: the culture, education, a person's temperament, all kinds of things. If you leave school at 16, by 18 you could have a stable working life and be a mature adult. If you are still a student at 28 or even 38, you may still have a lot of growing up to do! One obvious problem that we face in our society today is that adolescence now seems to extend well into the 30s, especially for some men. This is one reason that marriage is being delayed so long, far too long in many cases. Men, it is time to put the video games away, time to man up and grow up! God did not make us to be mummy's boys into our 20s and 30s; there is a time to grow up and be an adult and be responsible, be mature.

Of course, do not rush into marriage as though suddenly that is going to be a magic cure-all to make you mature and give you clarity and purpose in life if you are immature. The answer is to get serious about your grown-up life, get serious about your service to Christ so that you *can* enter marriage as a team, so you can be ready to serve as mutual helpers and not handicaps to one another. Our culture tells you to pamper yourself and procrastinate; God wants you to grow up and to get on with life. I think that in our contemporary culture both men and women need to wake up to that, but in my experience it is young men who sometimes need a hefty nudge, if not a sharp kick in the rear!

Three Do's. Now three Don'ts in this area, from the Bible's view of life.

Don't be too cautious

First, don't be too cautious. Do not be paralysed; it is important not to ignore cautions from others, and not to rush immaturely into relationships seeking answers to your problems, but do not ignore encouragement either! It was God who brought Adam his wife, so He was the original matchmaker. A helping hand from others is not to be despised. I do not mean frivolous matchmaking, but some people do need a nudge, because sometimes your friends can see things better than you. Sometimes they can see someone who would be an excellent helper for you.

Again, I think perhaps men more often need that nudge, even a healthy push. I needed that myself, I confess, and I am very glad I got it! I was being blind, stupid and far too slow but one of the elders of the church I was in as a young man came to me, and I will not tell you exactly what he said but it was a very strong nudge (to put it mildly), and I am still very thankful! Do not be too cautious and do not be paralysed. Don't despise a nudge or a hint from others who know you and love you, and especially from those who are a bit older and wiser. And that means that those who are older Christians must not be too cautious either. We must not be afraid to *give* a nudge or a push when it is required. I have found many young men today are as blind, or at least as slow, as I was, and my own thankful experience has given me the courage to kick a few posteriors into action – to the same happy result!

The Bible tells us not to be cautious, not to be always waiting. 'Cast your bread upon the waters' says the preacher (Eccles. 11:1), go ahead in faith and in trust, do not be too cautious. You can step out in trust when your God is a Sovereign God. When you are seeking first His kingdom, and His righteousness, you need not fear; He will not let your foot slip.

Don't be too cavalier

But second, don't be too cavalier either. Do not be so determined to find a partner that you snatch at what God is not giving. Do not have a cavalier, repetitive trial-and-error approach. A non-Christian may cycle through sexual relationships with multiple partners, but some Christians do much the same thing, just without it being sexual. But it is really not any more holy, or healthy, and it can be just as damaging.

Men especially have got to be careful: don't be a serial heart-breaker. Do not be cavalier with a female heart. It is very unimpressive to God and it is also unimpressive to other people. If you do find yourself in a relationship with a girl that does not work out – and there will be mistakes – then be very slow to make your next foray into the female affections. And if you are a friend of someone who has had a few failed relationships like that, then do urge caution, and some sober reflection, rather than just egging them on to the next pebble on the beach. Usually there are some important lessons they need to learn before they have another false start.

And I would say to the girls, do not aggressively chase men either. There is nothing so frightening to the male of the species than a woman on the hunt! Believe me, sensible blokes will run for their lives. Being a flirt might work, but there is a high chance that it will attract only the wrong kind of man, the sort of shallow person who will end up letting you down very badly, if not sooner then later.

But all of us: what the Bible calls us to is to go on serving God wholeheartedly, seeking first His kingdom in a healthy fellowship, a community of healthy Christian friendships in our church, or CU, or mission team or whatever. If we do that, wholeheartedly and contentedly, the rest will fall into place, if it is God's way for you. It usually will be, although not always – not all will marry. But God does know *your* needs.

Don't be too conspicuous

And so, thirdly, if you do find yourself drawn to someone, someone perhaps you serve with in church and you begin to form a relationship, let me say this: don't be too conspicuous. There is a seemly and helpful way to behave as a couple and there is an unseemly and an unhelpful way to behave, both for you and for other people.

Now, of course, it is wonderful to see healthy relationships forming in church. But what is not good is the damage that can be done by insensitivity, especially if a church witnesses people churning through lots of short-lived relationships. At worst, these can end up with people having to leave their church because they are so bruised at what has happened to them, especially if they see their former boyfriend or girlfriend publicly flaunting a new partner in church to everybody else. That is not honouring God and it is not loving one another. 'Do not use your freedom as an opportunity for the flesh but through love serve one another' is what Paul says (Gal. 5:13). We need to think of God, and we need to think of others in the church. We need to think what they *see*, what they will *assume*, and we need to think what *example* we are setting to younger ones, like our teenagers and to outsiders. We do not want to portray casual and cavalier attitudes to forming relationships. Far better to be discreet, so that by the time people cotton on to the fact that you are an 'item', you have a stable relationship that is going somewhere, not a flash in the pan that is going to end next week.

So do not be too cautious, but do not be cavalier either. And when things come together, do not be too conspicuous. If you are trusting, and if you are wise, and if you are real, then things will fall into place in the right way.

The road to marriage for the Christian is much less about the quest to find the right person than it is about a commitment to doing the right things. The Bible teaches that is the key at every stage, the answer to *every* problem, both before and in marriage itself: doing the right things God's way.

The greatest romance of all

But finally, you might think, is there no place for romance in all this? Well, of course there is! There is no place for the frothy, shallow nonsense of the Valentine's Day culture that we live in. That *is* all about worshipping relationships and seeking salvation in them. There is no place for that in a Christian view of marriage. But real romance? yes indeed! The gospel is *the* romance which all other true romance reflects. It is *the* story of love that we are all caught up in. The gospel is *the* love story, the only one, that will deliver and that does deliver, forever and ever, what our human hearts most need and seek.

As a Christian, the more you are taken up with the great romance, with love to the Lord Jesus Christ, with joy in extending *His* family, the more you will find others who share that love will become attractive to you – and vice versa. And you will find that is how the very best romantic bonds form with others who share the same joy and the same great goal in life that you do. Romantic love, erotic love that blossoms *that* way, is always the love that is real and that will last, because it is a love that outlasts life itself. And God is not perverse: He does not make us choose between godly marriage and fun marriage, or between marriage for love and attraction and marriage which submits to God but spends life with an ogre you cannot stand. Don't be so silly! God is your Heavenly Father; will He give you a stone or a snake when you ask Him for bread and fish (Matt. 7:9-11)?

No! When you seek His kingdom with all your heart, when you trust Him, you will find the helper you need, if indeed a marriage partner is what you need. And the helper you need will be the lover that you want, because that goal will be one. Marriage that serves Christ and His kingdom is, of all marriages, the most romantic and the most full of gladness and excitement and joy.

It is by thinking in this way, with biblical categories, and with Christian minds, that we reclaim the true place and purpose of marriage with all its joy. And in living this way, we shall also find the road to marriage far less tortuous and troublesome than we feared.

4. The Relationship of Marriage

There are only three passages in the New Testament that address commands specifically to husbands and wives: Ephesians 5:22-32, Colossians 3:18-19 which is very similar but less detailed, and 1 Peter 3:1-7. Each of these passages begins with the words: Wives, submit to your husbands.

In the old Scottish marriage service, Ephesians 5 is the first reading and it forms the very heart of the marriage service. In 1999, however, the Joint Liturgical Commission of Great Britain produced a new marriage service book for use by all denominations. It totally omits any mention of any of these three readings, the only ones in the Bible actually addressed to spouses! I think this simple fact illustrates eloquently the influence of secular feminism, not only on our culture but also on the church, since the second half of the twentieth century.

Of course, feminism did not arise in a vacuum. Male chauvinism is a very ugly thing, and it is right to resist it, especially for Christians, because the Bible is very clear that God has no truck with misogyny. To truly resist chauvinism and misogyny, and to promote relationships which truly liberate women – and men – means not disregarding the Bible, but taking it with the utmost seriousness.

But maybe you feel a bit uncomfortable when you read those words in Ephesians 5. Certainly, I notice when I read them at weddings there are titters going around – at best; sometimes you hear audible tutting, and see some rather angry faces.

Is that how we feel when we read these verses, even as Christians? If so, I think we need to be careful that *we* are not putting ourselves at the heart of marriage and banishing God to the periphery. Marriage is not an end in itself: it exists to serve the glory of God in the kingdom of Christ. When we forget that, we get into all sorts of confusion, which is especially dangerous if we are married ourselves. The Bible plainly teaches us that the *purpose* of marriage, indeed the ultimate purpose of our whole salvation in Christ, is what determines the *pattern* for godly marriage. Ephesians is a letter which makes this especially clear, because it is in the context of explaining God's ultimate purpose in salvation that we are given the ultimate pattern for marriage. So we need to examine its teaching carefully.

GOD'S ULTIMATE PURPOSE IN SALVATION

First of all, we need to be clear what the whole letter to the Ephesians teaches about God's ultimate purpose in salvation. It is nothing less than the re-creation through redemption of perfect harmony in the whole cosmos, the whole created order. Ephesians is full of the ultimate purpose of salvation and it has a great *future* focus.

We are of course told what we are saved *from* – 'Once you were dead in your trespasses and sins' (2:1). But there is a far greater emphasis on the present and future of God's redeemed people. '*But God*' is the transformative statement. 'But God...raised us up with him and seated us with him in the heavenly places in Christ Jesus so that in the coming ages he might show the immeasurable riches of his grace in kindness towards us in Christ Jesus' (2:4-7). And so now, 'we are his workmanship, created in Christ Jesus for good works which God prepared beforehand that we should walk in them' (2:10). This is what we are saved *for*. This is God's plan 'according to his purpose, which he set forth in Christ as a plan for the fullness of time, to unite all things in him, things in heaven and things on earth' (1:9-10).

Re-creation harmony

The gospel is about the complete re-creation of total harmony in God's created order, in heaven (the spiritual realm) and on earth, the world of humanity. It is the total reversal of the cosmic disaster of man's rebellion, which cursed the whole cosmos, and cursed all our relationships. Redemption is re-unifying into proper order the world as God created it to be, and has promised that it will be: a world in perfect harmony, of perfect relationships, all for the glory of the kingdom of our Lord Jesus Christ.

That is why, all through Ephesians, there is a great emphasis on oneness. Chapter 2 speaks about all in Christ Jesus now being brought together into one new society, and built together to become the dwelling place for God's Spirit. In chapter 3, Paul the Jew is speaking all about his mission to the gentiles, so that gentiles will be one with Jews, and that through this – the united harmony of one worldwide church – God's manifold wisdom will be displayed to all the hosts of heaven forever (3:10). This new and beautiful human harmony in Christ, between those once full of rivalry and strife, displays unmistakably the reversal of the rebellion and sin which so destroyed and disrupted this world. That is the calling of Christ's church for all eternity.

Walking in the love of Christ

Therefore, Paul says, we are to walk even now in a manner that is worthy of that calling (4:1). That means we must walk in love (5:2), walk as children of light, because we *are* now light in the Lord (5:8), and walk in God's own wisdom (5:15) understanding what the will of the Lord is (5:17). In other words, what he is saying is that every aspect of our lives, and every relationship, should demonstrate this re-creation harmony that God has wrought in Christ Jesus. So we are not to walk any longer in the ways of this fallen world, no longer as the pagans do, 'in the futility of their minds' (4:17). No, *we* are to be imitators of God. We are beloved children of His and therefore we are to walk as His children of light. In other words, we are to *be* the people we really are: 'filled with the Spirit' of His Son, the Lord Jesus (5:18).

> *be filled with the Spirit, addressing one another in psalms and hymns and spiritual songs, singing and making melody to the Lord with your heart, giving thanks always and for everything to God the Father in the name of our Lord Jesus Christ, submitting to one another out of reverence for Christ (Eph. 5:18-21).*

When Paul talks about the evidence of this Spirit-filled living, it is not some sort of ecstatic experience, or what we *feel*; he is talking about what we *do*, how we behave: how we 'walk in love'. This involves constantly encouraging one another in gospel truth, even in our song – 'speaking to one another in psalms and hymns and spiritual songs' (19).[1] It means 'giving thanks always and for everything' to God with all our hearts (20) – so Spirit-filled Christians are thankful people all of the time, not disgruntled, grumbling people. And, as verse 21 tells us, they are always 'submitting to one another out of reverence for Christ.'

Submitting in love to Christ

It is this last thing, this harmonious, mutual submission within our various relationships that Paul takes up and explains more fully in Ephesians 5:22-6:9. It is significant that he feels the need to apply this particular aspect of the Spirit-filled life before the conclusion of his letter, which of course is all about the real spiritual struggle with the powers of darkness we all face. It is no accident: these verses about submitting are all about the very real down-to-earth, day-to-day arena of life which is where real spiritual battles *are* played out in our lives. That is where the real spiritual battle rages.

---

1   Obviously Paul assumes Christian songs will not be trivial and lightweight but will have something worthwhile and substantial to say and teach.

It is in our everyday lives, in rubbing shoulders with one another in our relationships – husbands and wives, parents and children, masters and servants – that the Spirit-filled life needs to be in evidence. This is where the rubber hits the road, not when we are singing in church and everyone is smiling. It is when you go out on Monday morning, it is in the midst of real-life work, amid the reality of stress and strain in real families, that we are to demonstrate the re-creation harmony of God's new society. This is where we must show that all things in heaven and on earth are being united in Christ. As Christians we are all to submit to God's re-ordering of our sinful world and we are to demonstrate that harmony in all our relationships in life: that is our calling as the church. We are all called to show our submission to Christ as Lord by submitting to *His* ordering of relationships, not ours. And the first thing Paul has on his list is marriage.

> *submitting to one another out of reverence for Christ: wives, to your own husbands, as to the Lord...' (Eph. 5:21-22, my translation)*

Ephesians 5:21 is a hinge verse. In many modern Bibles verse 22 begins a new section under a heading, breaking the connection with verse 21, but in fact 5:21 is really the heading which governs each of the three examples that follow – relationships between wives and husbands, parents and children, and servants and masters. The standard Greek text indicates this with a comma at the end of verse 21, not a full stop (as in ESV), showing that the following verses fill out and expand what the 'submitting' looks like in various key relationships in life. Both *The Good News Bible* and Eugene Peterson's *The Message* recognise this and correctly put their heading for a new section above verse 21.

Three examples of 'mutual' submission

Seeing this immediately alerts us that some feminists, who want to interpret this verse differently, are forgetting the context of Paul's whole application. They accept verse 22 says, 'Wives submit to your own husbands,' but they say, 'Verse 21 says, "Submit *to one another*", so all that means is that wives are to submit to husbands, *and* husbands are to submit to wives in exactly the same way.' This, however, does not square with the text in its context. Paul clearly applies the principle giving three examples of mutual submission in relationships, not just one. They are parallel examples, each dealing with a relationship in which the way the parties relate to each other is plainly complementary, not absolutely symmetrical. Each side has its own individual and specific command as to how they are to submit to God's way in that relationship. Parents, for example, are not commanded to obey their children, as children are to obey their parents. There *is* a command to fathers, 'Do not provoke your children' but that is different; it is complementary submission, not identical (6:1-4). Similarly, servants are to obey their masters, doing good service 'as to the Lord, not man', and masters likewise are to '*do the same* to them' by showing no threatening; but that is how masters show their mutual submission 'out of reverence for Christ', not by obeying their servants (6:5-9).

When verse 21 says 'Submit to one another' it does not therefore mean that for godly mutual submission each party submits *in exactly the same way*. It simply means that each must submit to whom they ought to submit, in the appropriate manner of God's rightly ordered pattern.

Colossians 3:13 uses exactly the same 'one another' language in a slightly different context. Paul talks there about 'bearing with one another', and if one has a complaint against another, 'forgiving each other'. Obviously, forgiving one another does not mean that both parties do the forgiving. The wronged party forgives and the other one graciously receives that forgiveness. That is what forgiving one another means. Mutual forgiveness is complementary, not identical. Just so here. What submitting to one another means is spelt out in terms of what that means in each of these three relationships that follow. The appropriate role and the appropriate actions for each partner are spelt out in that relationship.

Harmonious interdependence restored

So there is mutuality in marriage, of course, as verse 21 implies. It is not – definitely not – a relationship of dominance, of one over the other. Nor is it a relationship of independence, of one from the other. But it *is* a relationship of inter-dependence, the one with the other, in the rightly ordered oneness of re-creation through redemption in Christ.

We must not lose sight of that; all of this about marriage is set in the context of the oneness of the harmony of all re-created relationships in Christ which serve the plan of God that God purposed in Christ before the foundation of the world. And these commands to husbands and wives are to serve that eternal purpose. Paul's theme all through Ephesians is that all we are is to be 'to the praise of his glorious grace' (Eph 1:6). That is the ultimate purpose of our salvation in Christ and therefore *that* is the ultimate purpose of our marriages.

So how is the *pattern* of our marriages to demonstrate God's ultimate purpose of recreated harmony in all relationships in His kingdom? How are we to walk worthily of our calling in true Christian marriage, walking not as the pagans, not in darkness but in wisdom as children of light?

GOD'S ULTIMATE PATTERN FOR MARRIAGE

This is what Ephesians 5:22-33 teaches us, by giving clear commands to both wives and husbands.

> *Wives, submit to your own husbands, as to the Lord. For the husband is the head of the wife even as Christ is the head of the church, his body, and is himself its Saviour. Now as the church submits to Christ, so also wives should submit in everything to their husbands.*
>
> *Husbands, love your wives, as Christ loved the church and gave himself up for her, that he might sanctify her, having cleansed her by the washing of water with the word, so that he might present the church to himself in*

splendour, without spot or wrinkle or any such thing, that she might be holy and without blemish. In the same way husbands should love their wives as their own bodies. He who loves his wife loves himself. For no one ever hated his own flesh, but nourishes and cherishes it, just as Christ does the church, because we are members of his body. 'Therefore a man shall leave his father and mother and hold fast to his wife, and the two shall become one flesh.' This mystery is profound, and I am saying that it refers to Christ and the church. However, let each one of you love his wife as himself, and let the wife see that she respects her husband (Eph. 5:22-33).

Paul is speaking here about the ultimate pattern for marriage, marriage that demonstrates re-creation through redemption in Christ. It is important to notice first of all that he is speaking here about *marriage* as a partnership in serving God. He is not speaking generally about men and women in society. Women are not commanded here to submit to men generally; wives submit to their *own* husbands, not everybody else's husbands.

There are two clear commands here, one to husbands and one to wives, and I want to summarise them in this way:

- Wives, says Paul, you are to be the helpers that God created you and redeemed you to be in your marriages.
- And husbands, we (I include myself) are to be the heads that God created us and redeemed *us* to be in our marriages.

However, we must be very clear what that *does* mean and what that does *not* mean.

Wives: be the helpers God created and redeemed *you* to be

'Wives, submit to your own husbands' says Paul in v22 and in case you miss it, he repeats the same thing to round off the paragraph, adding that they should submit 'in everything to their own husbands' (24). That is the general pattern that Paul is laying out for wives in the marriage relationship.

That verb 'submit' comprises a word meaning a sense of good order, as opposed to chaos, and to submit in this context means to gladly, and voluntarily, subject yourself to the right and proper order of God's will.[2] This state of affairs is God's good ordering for marriage, God's ordering as opposed to the chaos and the rivalry of non-submission.

The image is that of a team where the husband is the captain of the team. Now, that does not mean, the captain is the star of the team. Very often, indeed usually, that is not the case. Sometimes a rugby team captain is a prop forward, and they seldom score tries, and very rarely kick goals! Often you will not remember who the captain was.[3] Similarly in football: most of the stars and top goal scorers of the World Cup are not the team captains. So it does not mean that the husband is the *star* of the marriage team.

In very many marriages, certainly most that I know, the wife is the undoubted star! But it *does* mean that he carries the can when the chips are down. It does mean that he bears the final responsibility on his shoulders, as any team leader does, especially when things are really difficult. He is the one who must step up to the plate and take the pressure, and sometimes make that very tough call on behalf of the team. It does not mean a husband will never take advice or listen to his wife in such situations; he would be a fool if that were the case. But there are times when someone has to make the final call, and bear the consequences. That is what a husband must do as the leader of the marriage team, for the sake of his wife and family.

Many people today, especially women, still find this idea of submission difficult, so let us be clear about the rationale that Paul gives for this command. First of all, let us ask the question: why? Why should wives submit? Well, Paul gives two reasons.

---

2   See Ash, Christopher, *Marriage*, pp. 312-316 for a very helpful discussion of *taxis*, *hypotage* and *hypotasso* (the verb 'submit' here).

3   Of course, Scotsmen will never forget a Captain like David Sole who led Scotland to the Grand Slam against England at Murrayfield in 1990. But it took me a while to remember who was Captain in the 2018 Calcutta Cup triumph (John Barclay), while the dazzling star try-scorer Huw Jones was unforgettable.

God's good order for creation

First, because this is God's order for Creation, in order that marriage might serve and glorify His kingdom, 'for the husband is the head of the wife.' (5:23) He is taking us right back to Genesis and the purpose of man's creation as male and female in the beginning. Remember that God created mankind to serve His kingdom and to rule it and have dominion over all creation, but the male of the species proved inadequate on his own. (This at least is probably something most women will say 'Amen' to!) So God created Eve for Adam to be the suitable, complementary helper he needed. Adam came first as leader, as captain of the team, then Eve as helper – equal in status and dignity, yes indeed! That is exactly the point made in Genesis 2: any lesser creature was *not* suitable. She was of his own flesh, like him, and equal to him. But not equal in function. She does not compete with him, she complements him and completes him, and this is God's good ordering to make the human marriage team prosper.

But of course, read on and you find the events of Genesis 3 ruin all of that. What happens? Well, Eve sought to be the leader of the team, while Adam abdicated his responsibility and his leadership. It led to disaster, and you read in Genesis 3:16 of the curse that perpetuates that disordered relationship which both man and woman rebelliously chose for themselves. The woman's desire will be for her husband, to rule over him, but no, says God, he will rule over you. It is the right order, but sin will now make that whole relationship discordant and jarring, as it still is so much of the time. This explains the disharmony and battle of the sexes to this day: not harmonious interdependence but often disharmonious rivalry, wives not submitting but seeking to lead, and husbands very often not leading and rather feebly disengaging from the marriage team.

That is the way of the world. But not so with you! says Paul. We in the church are to display the New Creation way of restored harmony. Wives, be the helpers that God created you to be; that is how you will serve the kingdom and not oppose it. It is God's created pattern for our good.

God's glorious pattern for redemption

But secondly, Paul says, the reason you are to submit is because this is also God's pattern in redemption: 'for the husband is head of the wife, even as Christ is head of the church, his body, and is himself its Saviour' (23). Our marriages, he says, reflect *the great marriage* between Christ and His church.

When the New Testament speaks of Christ as the *head* over all things, it is quite clearly speaking of His rightful authority, His pre-eminence. Ephesians 1:22 tells us what that means: 'he put all things under his feet and gave him as head over all things to (or *for*) the church'. So Christ's headship does mean that all things are under His feet, that He is the authoritative ruler. But notice there is another sense in which Christ is head, because He is head to the church or, better, *for* the church. The church, His body, is enabled to enter into its destiny of dominion and rule in the heavenly realms because, and only because, Christ is the head *for* us. That is how we are raised up and seated with Him in the heavenly realms in Christ.

Christ's headship for His church is the source of its rich blessing; it is the conduit of our destiny and our salvation. Rich blessings flow from the head to the whole body so that it grows and reaches its destiny in Christ. That is the message of Ephesians 4. And in that same sense, too, the husband is to be the head of his wife. He is to be the leader into blessing, and into fulfilment in God's service, for his wife. And so in the light of that, just as the church submits to Christ gladly and joyfully, in order to be led into blessing, so wives are to submit to their husbands (5:24), because it is their road to blessing in Christ.

Paul does not say, does he, 'Husbands, forcefully subjugate your wives'? Not at all; rather he is saying, 'Wives, voluntarily, gladly submit to God's appointed way of blessing.' And this is why godly wives will want to submit: because it is God's pattern in redemption, it is His appointed way of blessing for your destiny.

But what does that mean? How are you to submit as a wife?

Submission is for Christ, and like Christ

Paul says 'submit *as to the Lord*' (22). He is saying submission is a privilege because it is not for your husband's sake, it is for the Lord's sake you are doing it. Maybe this is a help to you sometimes. It is not whether your husband *deserves* your willing submission; very often he does not, I am sure. The question is whether *Christ* deserves your submission to *His* path and to *His* command. This is a privilege, and not in any way something demeaning for you as a wife. It is not implying any inequality in status or any loss of dignity – absolutely the opposite. It is part of your submission to God's way, and that is a mark of being filled with the Spirit of God. In Romans 8:7-9, Paul says, 'the mind that is set on the flesh is hostile to God, for it *does not submit* to God's law... You, however, are not in the flesh but in the Spirit, if in fact the Spirit of God dwells in you.' And Christ's Spirit values and rejoices in submission to *His* head.

Paul explores this further in 1 Corinthians 11, where he talks of the head of every man being Christ, and the head of every wife being her husband, and the head of Christ Himself being God the Father. Christ is equal with God; He *is* God. There is no question of an inferior status of Christ the Son and yet He too has a head, the Father. And we read in 1 Corinthians 15 that the climax of the whole of the great story of redemption will come when Christ puts *Himself* into subjection under *His* head, God the Father. Jesus Christ delights to deliver the kingdom, His own kingdom, to God the Father. Everything is His, but He rejoices to subject Himself to *His* head, His heavenly Father.

So the Lord Jesus is the ultimate pattern for submission in marriage; He submits to God's perfect order in creation and redemption, and that pattern is the way of great blessing for us. It is a joyful surrender, made in order to serve the glory of the kingdom of Christ, and Paul says that this is the high calling of a Christian wife: submit to *your* head, your husband, *for the Lord* and for *His* sake. The greatest, the deepest, the most dignified fulfilling of your destiny, if you are a married woman, is to be the helper that God created you to be and redeemed you to be, in your marriage team. In that way your marriage will be 'to the praise of his glorious grace'; it is this pattern that serves God's ultimate purpose for you.

Is that a demeaning calling for any woman, to share in the pattern of the Lord Jesus Christ? Surely it cannot be – if it is the pattern of the Lord Jesus Christ Himself.

Husbands: be the head God created and redeemed *you* to be

At this point, many wives are very probably thinking, 'It is all very well to talk about joyful submission to husbands, emulating Christ's submission; the problem is, my husband is not like Jesus'. That is true. So those of us who are husbands need to listen, because we may be surprised by what Paul says next.

Many men in Ephesus, when they first heard these words read out, would have been very surprised at what came next. They would be expecting, 'Wives, submit to your husbands. Husbands, *keep your wives in submission*.' That would have been typical of the culture of that day, and it is typical of many macho and chauvinistic cultures still. Plenty of men the world over would be very happy to read, 'Wives, submit'. And happily think, 'Yes, I agree with that; let's enforce that: keep women in their place, under our control!' But if we think that is what it means, we are very, very wrong.

That kind of mistaken, authoritarian thinking shows us one reason why the feminist movement grew up in the first place – because of chauvinism of that kind, which is utterly unbiblical, and utterly unchristian. So men, we need to listen and be clear about what the Bible really says.

What is our instruction from God as husbands? Not 'rule your wives,' not 'disregard your wives,' not 'lord it over your wives and treat them as domestic help by day, and call-girls by night'. What does it say? 'Husbands, *love* your wives' (5:22). That is what headship means in marriage. That is the husband's part in this mutual submission that serves the kingdom of Christ.

'That is not too difficult', you may think. Most of us reckon we *do* love our wives: we give them flowers occasionally, we give them a cuddle now and again and say nice things, maybe compliment them on their new hair-do or clothes or whatever. Sometimes we even empty the dishwasher (there is love!) – at least we might if there are no glasses left in the cupboard and we have got blokes coming round to watch the football. 'We *do* love our wives.'

'No, no, no,' says Paul. 'I'm going to have to really explain this to you because most of you men just do not get it!' That is what Paul is doing in these verses that follow – He is teaching us what it *really* means to love your wives. Having addressed forty-five words to wives, Paul now addresses one hundred and fifteen words to husbands. It is quite a shock.

The pattern of headship

First, Paul focuses on the pattern of our headship as husbands, 'Love as Christ loved the church and gave himself up for her' (25). In case we are not clear what that 'giving up' means, recall 5:2 – that Christ gave Himself up as an offering, as a sacrifice to God, in a painful crucifixion. Just so men, we are to love our wives with self-giving, self-sacrificing, self-crucifying love that costs everything. Being head means *giving up everything* for the sake of your wife, in utter self-denial. That is a big blow to the chauvinistic ego. As C. S. Lewis puts it,

> *This headship, then, is most fully embraced not in the husband we should all wish to be, but in him whose marriage is most like a crucifixion; whose wife receives most and gives least, who is most unworthy of him, is – in her own*

mere nature – least loveable.... The chrism of this terrible coronation is to be seen not in the joys of a man's marriage but in its sorrows, in the sickness and suffering of a good wife or in the faults of a bad one, in his unwearying (never-paraded) care or his inexhaustible forgiveness.[4]

That is what real headship is about: loving as Christ, the real Man, loved His church, giving up *everything* for her. It is the team captain who shoulders everything when the chips are down, who bears it all when the team is up against it.

So, men, is that how we are loving our wives? If not, I wonder if perhaps that is why many wives find it very hard to bear this command to submit. C. S. Lewis goes on to say that no feminist should ever grudge the husband this crown of headship, because it is not a crown of gold, it is a crown of thorns. He then says so very penetratingly, 'the real danger is not that husbands may grasp this crown too eagerly; but that they will allow or compel their wives to usurp it.'[5]

Is that not true? Who is the real burden-bearer in most marriages, men? Who really bears the cross? Who suffers the loss? Who is it who is constantly giving themselves up for the marriage, for the family, for the home? All too often, even in Christian marriages, the truth is that it is not us, but our wives. 'Come on, men,' says Paul, 'Be *real* men: love your wives as Christ loved the church.' That is the pattern of real headship in marriage.

The purpose of headship

But there is more. Verses 26-28 speak clearly about the purpose of that headship. Christ sacrificed Himself that He might bring His body the church into its God-ordained destiny, to present it holy and in splendour and radiant glory forever. And so, '*in the same way*, husbands should love their wives as their own bodies' (28).

---

4   Lewis p. 128.

5   Lewis p. 129.

We men are to sacrifice everything about ourselves in order to love our wives, and to do so in such a way as to bring them into their personal destiny of splendour and glory in Christ forever. If you are a married man, this is the purpose of your love for your wife. It is not about your self-fulfilment, it is about *her* fulfilment. It is about the full flowering of your wife in holiness and grace and glory in Jesus Christ. Is that ever even on our minds as husbands, let alone in our thinking about headship in marriage? But that is the purpose of a truly Christ-like loving headship in marriage, according to Paul.

He goes on to add real persuasion to his command to love this way as Christ-like heads. Not only can our wives only attain *their* true destiny in Christ through our loving of them this way, the same is true for ourselves. 'He who loves his wife loves himself. For no one ever hated his own flesh'; he looks after it, he nourishes it so it grows and develops (5:28-9). Marriage has united husband and wife into one flesh (31), and that means you cannot grow your *own* spiritual destiny without your wife growing into *hers*, because you are one.

But she cannot grow unless you will be the head for her that Christ wants you to be, unless you will lead her into that destiny. There is something very profound about all this – Paul says that plainly 'This mystery is profound' (5:32) – not incomprehensible, but a wonderful and a glorious thing now made known by God in the gospel. [6] The wonder is that our marriages, in their one-flesh union, reflect the union of Christ with His church. And therefore we can only grow individually in Christ if we grow *together* in Him.

In Ephesians 4:15-16 Paul says we all, in the church, grow up into Him who is the head (Christ) and from Him the whole body, the whole church, grows *as each part does its work*. And it is just the same in marriage: growth towards our destiny in Christ happens only when each part works properly, when each partner in the marriage works harmoniously; wives helping, not hindering, and husbands leading

---

6   This is what 'mystery' means all through Ephesians: unsearchable riches once hidden, now brought to light. See for example Ephesians 3:9.

with love – real, sacrificial, cross-shaped love. Only thus, together, will you grow into your true destiny in Christ. 'He who loves his wife loves himself' too, says Paul, to that end. But if you do not love your wife, then you damage not only your wife but yourself also. This is what it means to be one flesh. If one spouse hurts, so does the other, just like in the church. We are one body: if one part hurts, so does the other, if one is blessed, so will the other be.

The beauty of headship

Do you see what a wonderful and beautiful pattern of partnership this really is? There is not a sniff of ugly male chauvinism about it; rather, it is the very opposite.

Any man who stresses the idea of dominance, or who thinks in terms of subjugating his wife, is a hundred miles away from the Bible's pattern here. And any woman who would resist this true pattern of Christ-like headship, in terms of godly leadership into a radiant destiny in Christ, she too is far away from God's great purpose for her. But when a Christian couple does embrace gladly a marriage like this, then not only will it be for their greatest blessing and furthering of *their* eternal destiny in Christ, it also manifestly serves the kingdom in so many other ways too. Paul says something of the beauty and the pattern of the glory of Christ will also shine forth from them into the world, on earth and even in heaven.

Marriage is to the praise of His glorious grace, marriage showcases the purpose of God in Creation and redemption, marriage preaches the gospel of grace in a visible way. And how desperately our world needs to see that in real Christian marriages! Paul reminds us that our world is darkened in understanding, alienated from the life of God because of ignorance, hard-hearted, callous, given up to sensuality (4:18). Alas, that so often describes relationships in our culture today.

But marriage lived truly for God, His way, speaks of real love, real commitment, real sacrifice – all for one glorious purpose in Christ, that will shine light into the darkness of this dark world. Just by being this way, Christian marriage will preach the grace and the mercy of God and the promise of God in Christ to all who will embrace Him. This, says Paul, is what every Christian married couple is called to.

At the end of the passage Paul concludes, 'Let each one of you love' like this. Husbands, love like this, *like* Christ; wives, respect your husband *for* Christ (33). Each one, he says; not just some, not just those marriages that seem to be always naturally easy relationships (although I doubt if there are any of those in reality). As the whole body of the church grows when each part does its work, so also the witness of real marriage today needs each Christian marriage to do its work and shine: not just by thinking this way, but actually *doing* it this way.

Marriages that show Christ to the world

That is hard because we are fallen creatures. We are not yet liberated from sin's presence. But 'grace was given to each one of us' (Eph. 4:7). God commands us to walk worthily of our calling – and when God commands, He gives grace to obey. His commands are, at the same time, His gracious enablings. We must obey Him, but by His grace we *can* obey Him. So let each one who is married walk worthily in their own marriage, and let everyone encourage marriage in others which reflects this ultimate pattern.

Wives: be the helpers God made you to be and redeemed you to be. It will be hard at times, no doubt sometimes very frustrating. You may have to help your husband to be the leader God has called him to be. For some of you that will be very difficult, and perhaps painful, and you will need to ask the Lord to help you with the grace and strength you need. But remember, you are not doing it first for your husband, but for your Lord, and He is the God of *all* grace who will Himself strengthen you (1 Pet. 5:10).

Husbands: be the head – the loving leader to glory – that God made us to be and redeemed us to be. The chief responsibility is ours if there are wrong, damaging patterns in our marriage; as captain, we carry the can. Sometimes there is unworthy chauvinism and boorishness among men, even Christian men – yes, even in evangelical churches. That demands repentance and real change: we must depart from any whiff of that. But more often there is lazy, and frankly wimpish, abdication of responsibility. That is how we men are by nature: retreating into a comfortable world of work, or the newspapers, or sport, or the pub, or a computer, or whatever else it is – leaving all the real yoke of responsibility on our wives, while we get on with loving ourselves. Well, 'Let each one love his wife as himself', says Paul, because that is the only love that will lead either of you to your true destiny in Christ. When I worked in London, most Monday mornings, an older minister, Dick Lucas who was himself a bachelor used to come into my office to discuss the weekend. I relished our chats, but nearly every week he would say to me: 'Are you loving your wife?' I used to get quite annoyed – because he said it so often! But the truth was, I needed to hear it; and I still do. I suspect most husbands reading this book do, too.

So let us listen to God's commands to us, both husbands and wives (and prospective husbands and wives too) so that none of us in marriage will be grieving the Spirit of God. Husbands, 'Let each one of you love his wife as himself'; and surely that will motivate any wife to 'see to it that she respects her husband.'

This is the way of blessing which will light up your life together; but it is also the way of beauty which will light up the darkness of our lost world. Marriage was created by God, and redeemed for us in Christ, so that people might see something on earth so beautiful that it speaks eloquently of the greatness of God's love, and the joyful purpose of His grace in winning a bride for his Son. May that be our vision for married life: that people will see our lives of glad and rightly ordered partnership, serving Christ together as one, and something of the beauty and mystery of Christ's redeeming love will shine forth to them. May our Christian marriages be ones that preach the gospel of grace just by what they are!

5. The Rupture of Marriage

The Bible does not hide the truth that ours is a fallen world, and the essence of that fallenness is seen in the ruptured relationships which dominate human life. The breach of mankind's covenant bond of faithfulness to God lead to rifts in every other kind of human relationship – national, international, ethnic, social and personal, and the deepest and most personal rupture we know is that at the heart of the family, the rupture of the marriage bond itself. So we cannot avoid some discussion on how we are to think as Christians when the marriage bond may seem in grave danger of being broken, or indeed a marriage has already broken apart. We all know that relationship and family breakdown is a great scourge in our contemporary society.[1] Very sadly, we also know that it is also a reality in the church, and so we must face up to this and seek the Bible's guidance.

This whole area is complex and difficult on many levels. For many, it is also hard and painful to read about, and that makes it hard also to write about. Some difficulties, because these are such personal issues, are much better dealt with in private conversations with your minister. There are also areas I cannot possibly cover in one brief chapter, and there will be issues you may need to discuss further with others. And, since our focus in this book is on healthy loving – love and marriage

---

1   I have already referred to some of the grim statistics in chapter 1 & 2.

as it should be – I do not want it to become unbalanced by speaking disproportionately about divorce and marital rupture, a subject on which many (often long) books have been written.[2] But there is basic and very clear teaching in the Bible which is essential for us all to understand as Christians, and I hope that by dealing with some of this, it will help us all to be able to both give help to, and seek help from, one another in a biblically informed and compassionate way. We cannot avoid some hard work and close attention to the Bible text here. I want to focus on 1 Corinthians 7 since this is a chapter which does give clarity to some of the main issues involved with marriage strain and breakup. Paul writes,

> *Now concerning the matters about which you wrote: 'It is good for a man not to have sexual relations with a woman.' But because of the temptation to sexual immorality, each man should have his own wife and each woman her own husband. The husband should give to his wife her conjugal rights, and likewise the wife to her husband... Do not deprive one another, except perhaps by agreement for a limited time, that you may devote yourselves to prayer; but then come together again, so that Satan may not tempt you because of your lack of self-control (1 Cor. 7:1-3, 5).*

We must remember, of course, that Paul is not writing here (or anywhere else for that matter) a treatise on marriage, but a letter to a church in a particular time and place. Two things help illuminate his teaching.

Sexual confusion in the church

First, as verse 1 indicates, this letter is part of an ongoing correspondence with this church, made necessary because it was very mixed-up on a whole host of issues – including a great deal of wrong thinking and wrong behaviour in the area of sexual relations and marriage. Hence

2   For a book dealing in detail with exegesis on all the biblical passages relating to divorce, I would suggest John Murray, *Divorce* (P & R, 1961), and for a very readable and pastorally sensitive book looking at all the practical issues involved with great sanity, *Divorce*, by Frank Retief (Christian Focus Publications, 1995).

the long section of 1 Corinthians 5-7 was written. Chapter 5 tells us that a form of incest, shameful even among the pagans, was being arrogantly tolerated in the church. Chapter 6 says others were using prostitutes and apparently justifying that by saying, 'Well, it is just a bodily matter, not something that could ever taint us spiritually.' Paul also reminds us that members of the church had a background of adultery, homosexuality and other sexual immorality. But it seems from the beginning of chapter 7 that some others had gone to the very opposite extreme, perhaps in reaction to all that was going on. They had written to Paul saying surely therefore people should stop all sexual activity, even between husbands and wives: 'It is good for a man not to have sexual relations with a woman' at all! Is that the higher and better way for real Christians in the face of such immorality?

According to the Corinthian elite perhaps, this was the way – absolute celibacy. And of course, down the history of the church there have been those who have advocated this; that is one reason why there are convents and monasteries and so on. But Paul the apostle is having none of it. No, he says, a man should go on having sexual relationships *with his own wife* and vice versa: not with prostitutes, or with someone else's wife, and certainly not with your father's wife or with other men. Marriage is the answer to immorality, and marriage needs sex, so do not shrink back from your marital responsibilities! The only possible reason for 'fasting' from sexual relations, is for a time of prayer. Even that, he says, must be short, and even that is 'a concession, not a command'. So it is extraordinary that the apostle Paul is so often derided for being anti-sex, when he is quite the opposite. Real piety for a Christian couple in marriage, says Paul, is a regular sex life, *not* extended prayer times!

It is often said today that society has changed so greatly from the time of the Bible, and so the church too must change because traditional ideas of marriage no longer work. But that just does not hold up when we think of Corinth. This was, even by our standards today, a very sexually 'progressive' society, promiscuous and 'liberated', as some would say. The church, too, had imbibed a lot of that sexual confusion, but Paul's message, spoken in a context not at all dissimilar to our world today, was very clear: 'No, you are not to be as the pagan world round about you. You are to be holy. You are to use God's gifts as He commands them, not just as you please.' That is just as important for us to understand today.

Crisis times in the world

Paul also writes into a specific situation, at a time he calls in 7:26 'the present distress.' There was food shortage due to widespread famine in the known world, with related social unrest, and probably disease was also rife as a result, causing a general sense of distress; we know there had been a spate of recent illnesses and deaths in the church at Corinth, perhaps related to this situation, yet also in some way related to the sinful behaviour of some of the believers (11:30). So no doubt there was a great deal of uncertainty and even fear among many. It is understandable in a time of crisis like that the many Christians would be saying, 'What should we be doing?' What about those betrothed to be married, and wondering, 'Should we go ahead and get married, and start families, or not? There will more mouths to feed, how will we cope in this time of crisis?' And for those widowed, what about remarriage?

These are the kind of issues Paul deals with in 7:25-38, and this 'crisis' context explains why in much of what he says, particularly in this second half of the chapter, he gives advice, not clear commands. He gives his judgment about what is best, and yet insists they will not be sinning if they do differently, because it is a matter of pragmatic wisdom in the present situation of crisis. But what all believers need, especially in times of crisis, is perspective: detachment from all the things of this world which one day will pass away, even marriages. Hence, all the way through chapter 7, Paul is focusing minds on the bigger issue of eternity; it is the call of eternity which must colour the Christian's thinking about all matters of merely passing earthly relationships, for 'the present form of this world is passing away' (v. 31).

What matters is the eternal kingdom of Christ, because that is everlasting. So Paul wants them to be 'free from anxieties' about all these lesser things (32), and secure about what really matters: whatever you do what I really want is your 'undivided devotion to the Lord' (v. 35). That means they can be pragmatic about many issues; in the current situation, choosing not to marry may spare you domestic burdens and anxieties, but if you choose to marry that is fine, just do not let that hinder your devotion to the Lord. And so on.

Very importantly, however, even when he teaches this pragmatic approach for a time of crisis, and despite his frequent emphasis on wisdom rather than commands, on the issue of rupturing marriages which are already in existence – on the issue of separation and abandoning marriages – Paul is exceptionally clear. He does not just give wise advice, but clear commands. He makes it very evident that the sanctity of the marriage bond must not ever, even in difficult circumstances, be diminished or downplayed for Christian people.

NOT RUPTURE, BUT RECONCILIATION

First of all Paul addresses married Christians and his message is simple: when troubles come, do not think rupture, think reconciliation. Christian believers are not to contemplate marriage break-up. Rather they must seek God's grace for reconciliation.

> *To the married I give this charge (not I, but the Lord): the wife should not separate from her husband (but if she does, she should remain unmarried or else be reconciled to her husband), and the husband should not divorce his wife (1 Cor. 7:10-11).*

There is no significant difference between the words 'separate' and 'divorce' here. Separation just means decisive leaving, it means the rupture of the marriage, legalised or not. Neither party should ever countenance rupture of the marriage bond; this is not advice, it is Paul's clear apostolic command – do not contemplate that, ever. The parenthesis in v11 is not a get-out; he is not giving an exception here, as though to say 'don't divorce, except if you are happy to then remain unmarried.' What he is saying in brackets is simply recognising that this is a fallen world, and that Christians are sinful and there are situations where that rupture has already, wrongfully, happened. He is merely providing for the regulation of a situation that *has* happened, even though it should not have. He is not giving release as a way out for somebody who wants that to happen.

This is the clear apostolic command: no Christian couple should ever, ever enter marriage thinking that separation and divorce will be a potential way out for them if things go wrong. No Christian married couple should pursue divorce thinking that is a sin-free option for ending things. Certainly there is to be no dreaming of remarriage; Paul is very clear – if the worst does happen, then there is still no release. The only options he gives here are reconciliation or remaining unmarried, seeking no further marriage union. That is Paul's authoritative apostolic charge.

The word of the Lord

Of course, this is the direct teaching of Jesus also – Paul says he is giving a charge specifically from the Lord (v. 10). What does he mean? Here is what Jesus said in Matthew 5:31-32,

> It was also said, 'Whoever divorces his wife, let him give her a certificate of divorce.' But I say to you that everyone who divorces his wife, except on the ground of sexual immorality, makes her commit adultery, and whoever marries a divorced woman commits adultery.

According to Jesus here the only possible grounds of divorce and remarriage is 'sexual immorality'; the Greek word is 'porneia', which means gross sexual infidelity against a spouse. Again, the exception is not a get-out clause; obviously no Christian can ever imagine,

'I want out of my marriage, so let me commit adultery' as a way out. Notice that Jesus speaks of divorce and remarriage together, because divorce implies that normally remarriage will take place; improper divorce alone cannot make someone an adulterer, it is the subsequent remarriage that does that. Jesus assumes divorce legally releases for remarriage (we shall come back to this point later). So, it is very clear Paul is just passing on what Jesus says – no divorce.

In Matthew 19, Jesus repeats this clear teaching, and He explains why: as we have already seen, it goes right back to creation.

> *And Pharisees came up to him and tested him by asking, 'Is it lawful to divorce one's wife for any cause?' He answered, 'Have you not read that he who created them from the beginning made them male and female, and said, "Therefore a man shall leave his father and his mother and hold fast to his wife, and the two shall become one flesh"? So they are no longer two but one flesh. What therefore God has joined together, let not man separate.' They said to him, 'Why then did Moses command one to give a certificate of divorce and to send her away?' He said to them, 'Because of your hardness of heart Moses allowed you to divorce your wives, but from the beginning it was not so. And I say to you: whoever divorces his wife, except for sexual immorality, and marries another, commits adultery' (Matt. 19:3-9).*

God has made husband and wife 'one flesh', and so 'what therefore God has joined together, let not man separate'. It is not that the marriage bond is *impossible* to break. This is the teaching of Roman Catholicism, but that cannot be so because, for one thing, death does break the bond, and God can allow the bond to be sundered, as Jesus says, where there is adultery. People, too, can sinfully break it, which is precisely why Jesus warns us not to. He cannot warn us to do something if it is impossible, but Jesus is plain – no divorce. His opponents say, well, 'Why then did Moses command arrangements for divorce?'[3] Jesus

---

3   The Pharisees are referring to Deuteronomy 24:1-4, a law which does not command divorce, but does insist that if a man *does* get rid of his wife he cannot leave her to be destitute, or exploited, or become defiled through being treated like a chattel. He must make sure she is protected. The law was to stop men

replies that Moses *allowed* it and he made processes to regulate it, even though it should never have been, because of sin: 'because of your hard hearts'. But it was never God's design. The Pharisees are so typical of human beings: immediately we want to look for loopholes. We are all like accountants by nature, who as soon as there is a tax law, look for the loophole. 'So what way *can* you get a divorce, Jesus, and still feel righteous?' But Jesus says, 'No, no, no. Let us get right back to the real issue, the sanctity of marriage.'

We need to be very careful not to be like the Pharisees in our thinking in this whole area of divorce, seeking loopholes to justify what we may want to do. Jesus says from the beginning it was not so, and the implication is that it must not be so in His kingdom of re-creation. Followers of Jesus are to think marriage not divorce, and reconciliation not rupture.

Absolute clarity

There can be no question about the clarity, or the absoluteness, of Jesus' teaching here. Even the disciples are very sober about it: they say in response, 'If such is the case of a man with his wife, it is better not to marry.' Yet Jesus says, 'Not everyone can receive this saying, but only *those to whom it is given*' (19:10-11). So it is not impossible for marriage to be as God wants it to be: solid and lasting. Jesus has already said to His own followers 'To *you it has been given* to know the secrets of the kingdom of heaven' (Matt 13:11, emphasis mine) and marriage is one of the things given us in order to serve that kingdom. I take it Jesus means that Christian marriage, marriage in surrender to Him,

---

from committing an 'abomination before the Lord' or bringing 'sin on the land' of God's inheritance. The very next verse shows that not only does God want marriage to be protected, but positively *promoted*: a newlywed man is exempted from public service for a year in order to 'be free at home to be happy with the wife whom he has taken'. A better translation may be, to '*make happy*' the wife whom he has taken! (Deut. 24:5).

is the very marriage that can, and must, display the unbreakable re-creation harmony of the 'new world' to which He is leading us.[4]

Coming back to 1 Corinthians chapter 7, it is clear that Paul is not dealing with circumstances where adultery has taken place, but with other situations. He is saying that for Christians there should be no separation, no abandoning marriage, and no looking for an easy way out, instead you are to seek God's grace for reconciliation (7:11).

That must always be the aim of any Christian couple in difficulties, and of the church in seeking to help. And there *is* grace, there is grace that works through you, if you are seeking God's way, grace to reconcile problems long before the issue of separation becomes an issue – and even afterwards, Paul says here. Even if it has already happened, there can still be reconciliation.

NOT RUPTURE, BUT REDEMPTION

Paul then goes on to address another group that he calls 'the rest,' and addresses the situation of a believer who is married to an unbeliever, most likely somebody who has come to faith but whose spouse has not become a Christian. And he says even there, do not think rupture, think redemption.

To the rest I say (I, not the Lord) that if any brother has a wife who is an unbeliever, and she consents to live with him, he should not divorce her. If any woman has a husband who is an unbeliever, and he consents to live with her, she should not divorce him. For the unbelieving husband is made holy because of his wife, and the unbelieving wife is made holy because of her husband. Otherwise your children would be unclean, but as it is, they are holy. But if the unbelieving partner separates, let it be so. In such cases the brother or sister is not enslaved. God has called you to peace. For how do

---

4   The whole of Matthew 19 is about following Jesus His way, now, surrendering and letting His Kingdom way define all this world's relationships, so that we shall inherit with Him 'the new world', literally the 'regeneration' (19:28) and receive eternal life.

you know, wife, whether you will save your husband? Or how do you know,
husband, whether you will save your wife? (1 Cor. 7:12-16).

Paul says a believer, even in a difficult marriage with an unbeliever, must
not seek break-up. They are to seek God's grace for the redemption of
their spouse (7:16), and even if that does not happen, that does not
justify a divorce. Again, this shows how powerful the marriage bond
really is. Paul is still speaking authoritatively here; this is not advice,
but a command, though he cannot quote Jesus directly because this
was a later situation created by the church's mission. It is a point worth
noting that mission creates many problems when people are converted
out of pagan life, and the more converts the more mess to be sorted out
in people's lives. Real mission can be really messy! Churches often do
not cope easily with mess and some Christians are the same; they want
to protect their consciences from defilement, and so it is no surprise
that these are rarely people up to their eyeballs in evangelism. A holy
huddle is much more comfortable than a messy church engaged in
mission.

But mission creates many messy situations, with all sorts of baggage
from people's backgrounds. So what are we to do? Maybe some
over-pious Corinthians were worried about defilement, about being
a believer, but attached in this intimate bond with someone who is
a pagan. Perhaps they had been reading in the Old Testament how
mixed marriages caused such disaster among the people of God, and
were thinking, 'Surely I must break from this marriage'. Or maybe they
were just feeling the real struggle of being married now as a Christian
to a non-Christian spouse. It is very understandable, and I have known
people today who experience that struggle, and wonder perhaps if it
would be easier to have a fresh start with a Christian. But no, says Paul,
the marriage bond is sacred. Do not divorce on these grounds. As long
as your spouse is willing to live with your faith, do not be the one to
end the marriage.

Grace works in families

He has a wonderfully positive reason for this; it is not that you are defiled by your pagan spouse, it is the reverse: they are 'made holy' by you (v. 14)! Paul does not mean they will automatically be saved; in verse 16 he says they cannot be certain of that. But what he does mean is that their spouse has been brought into the orbit of God's saving grace at work in the world through His church, and to all the privileged opportunities that brings. Clearly this is the case for the children of even one believing parent (v. 14); it is a given for them that their children are not treated as 'unclean' pagans, but 'holy', privileged heirs of God's grace who are set apart from the world to be raised in the faith for Christ as part of the church. None of them disputes that is so for their children, and Paul says that by God's gracious providence an unbelieving spouse, too, has been granted great privilege by God; they are brought near to His grace.

This is such an important thing to grasp if you have become a Christian, but your spouse has not. In a marriage like this, God's Spirit has already invaded the household. He is already at work in grace in your family, and your spouse may thus be won for the Lord Jesus. It is not a guarantee, not magic; God is sovereign. But it is a word of hope: your spouse may indeed be saved precisely this way; it may be God's very plan for them. God works in families. It is the same today too; I have seen it happen, even when it has taken a very long time, many years, for a non-Christian partner to gradually be drawn in to the life of the church, through the patient and prayerful witness of their Christian spouse, and, indeed, through that of their children.

So not only is there reason to preserve marriage just because it is part of His Creation, part of His common grace for the health of all mankind, and therefore a sacred covenant, but also because God's redeeming grace works through marriage and family life. This should always be your goal, even in the struggles of that kind of mixed marriage. It can be very hard at times, but if that is where you are, then cling on to this good news! See the eternal perspective of God in your marriage, not just the struggles of today. God is at work, and who knows how far that might go? Who knows just how deep that influence of grace might be in your beloved husband or your beloved wife? So do not think rupture, think redemption. There is grace to be found for redemption when the Spirit of God is at work.

NOT PREOCCUPATION, BUT PEACE

But sometimes it just does not turn out like that, and when an unbelieving spouse does separate, when a believer is abandoned by an unbeliever, Paul's message is: you must not be preoccupied but you must be at peace. If that happens, 'let it be so' (7:15). A decisive end has come and that must be accepted and not resented. Why? Because 'God has called you to peace', not to preoccupation, not to anxiety, not to guilt, not for an ongoing feeling of responsibility in those circumstances. As the believer, you are not to seek the break-up of a marriage like that, but if your unbelieving spouse does, you are to accept it and to be at peace.

It is a very common thing for a Christian spouse to feel a great burden of responsibility in that situation – for the marriage, for their spouse, even for their salvation. But Paul says you must entrust that to God and be at peace. This may be a word that you, or a Christian friend or family member of yours, needs to hear if that has been the situation. I think the same principle would also hold today for a *de facto* marriage, a couple living together in a sexual relationship and when one becomes a Christian the other will not tolerate it. It is similar when one spouse drifts away and abandons their Christian faith, and their Christian family, as very sadly does sometimes happen. Paul says that such a person, having denied the faith, 'is worse than an unbeliever' (1 Tim. 5:8). Where that happens there will often be shock and great sadness in the church, but Paul says you are not to let this burden you with guilt. Let it be so, for God has called you to peace, and His grace will grant you that, and hope for the future.

Paul also says that in this situation the abandoned spouse 'is not enslaved' (7:15). It is very different from what he says in verse 11. There they must remain unmarried, but here they are not enslaved; the implication is that remarriage here is possible. There has been, in God's eyes, a sad, but now legitimate divorce, a decisive end to that marriage: Let them go – 'Let it be so' – and be at peace. In this specific situation, for a believer whose marriage is ruptured by an unbelieving spouse, probably largely because of their faith – not just any old divorce, and not one deliberately brought about by the believer – Paul says, there is grace to allow a new beginning in remarriage. They are no longer bound – 'enslaved' – by the marriage bond, just as a widow is no longer bound; 'if her husband dies she is free to be married to whom she wishes, only in the Lord' (7:39). Of course, this same caveat holds true here too: there is no question of a Christian, having been once in a marriage with an unbeliever to be free to go and marry another unbeliever – that *would* be wilful sin (see also 2 Cor. 6:14).

There are, of course, many more things that could be said about divorce and remarriage, but this is the basic essence of the Bible's position. It is very clear, even though it may not be easy. But let me try to draw some implications for how we are to think about and deal with various situations we shall encounter as Christians in the church today.

If you are a married Christian, do not consider divorce

Are you a married Christian like me, or a soon-to-be married Christian? What are we supposed to think? Well, that divorce is just not an option for us to be contemplating, and that is that. It is not something to have on our radar as we enter marriage, nor when we begin to encounter the inevitable stresses and strains which are a normal part of every marriage. In some situations, of course, that might be very hard, and there may be a lot of help needed, but the apostle's command is very clear. It is also Jesus' command. There can be no such thing, according to the Bible, as a no-fault divorce for a believer. We just must not begin even to think in this way.

There is a striking scene in the blockbuster Netflix series *The Crown*, when Her Majesty the Queen and Prince Philip are discussing a crisis in their relationship in the early years of marriage, caused by the (almost) impossible pressures of such a Royal marriage. With the conflicting duties for the Queen as a wife, and mother, and as Head of State, and all these extraordinary demands upon her shoulders, not to mention the constant public scrutiny, it is not hard to imagine a marriage more likely to fail.

But we hear the Queen say to her husband, 'The exit route which is open to everyone else' – divorce – 'it's not an option for us.' And because it is simply not something they can even contemplate, they set about working out their marriage, which has now passed its seventieth anniversary. How many more marriages would have lasted the distance, had not divorce become so much easier today?

The question for us is, 'do you trust the Lord Jesus to know what is best for you for your life and for your marriage?' If we do, we too shall be people who begin marriage, and continue through marriage, knowing that 'the exit route which is open to everyone else is not an option for us.' The Lord Jesus wants us to think marriage, not divorce; always.

And yet the truth is, in this still-suffering world, and in our still-sinful lives, even as Christians we may find ourselves in a place we do not want to be, and ought not to be. We cannot turn the clock back. It may be that things have broken down in your marriage – or are breaking down. Well, there *is* good news in this passage. Paul says there is grace available for believers; reconciliation is possible. If both are willing to humble themselves and to ask for Jesus' help and the help of Jesus' people, nothing is impossible with God. If you are married as a Christian you must believe that, pray for that, and work for that.

But sometimes that does not happen. Sometimes things are just too far gone and separation has already occurred, perhaps ultimately having been the lesser of two evils; the marriage has ended, for whatever reason. Paul does not offer remarriage as an option in this case; rather, we are to pray for grace for reconciliation, but if not, grace for contentment to remain unmarried.

If you are a Christian and your spouse is not: there is hope!

What about the converted Christian spouse and the non-Christian husband or wife? Well, there is hope also, hope for grace, for redemption. You do not know what God's wonderful love can do, so work at your marriage, pray, trust God; who knows what God will do in your unbelieving spouse's life? Faith can be very contagious in families. A friend of mine who had a vague Christian background, but was never really committed, married a man with no Christian influence at all, indeed very sceptical. But she was then truly converted through a local evangelical church. Imagine the joy I witnessed some time later, in seeing her husband, now professing faith, and their two young boys being baptised together! Twenty years on, that whole family (now six) are still solidly serving the Lord together.

Often today it is not an actual marriage partner, but a cohabiting partner who is converted, and I think these verses here apply in just the same way; you do not have to depart just because you have become a Christian and your partner has not; effectively you are living as husband and wife. As a Christian now, of course, you will want to regularise that relationship in marriage and make it proper in God's eyes. It may be your desire to do this which forces a crisis: your unbelieving partner realises that your faith is serious, and will impact your life, and they do not want that, so they walk out on you – that can happen. But, it might also be the path to faith, to salvation, to redemption.

I remember one woman who was wonderfully converted, and who brought her partner of many years along to the next Christianity Explored course. He only came because he was so furious at her new-found faith that he was determined to show her how wrong it all was, and, like Saul of Tarsus, he came breathing threats and curses. But, also like Saul, he too met the Risen Lord Jesus.

There was quite a bit of untangling of things in order to regularise their relationship as a proper marriage, but they did, and continued to serve the Lord faithfully together as one. But in the circumstances someone is abandoned by an unbelieving partner, Paul says they are not bound; there is grace for a new start, for remarriage, or for the first real and proper marriage.

After adultery, there is grace for a new start

If you are a Christian and your marriage has been destroyed by adultery, whether your spouse was a professing Christian or not, there is, in God's grace, opportunity for a new start. Jesus does not say that remarriage after divorce due to marital infidelity constitutes adultery, implying that re-marriage is possible. But even in these sad circumstances, that new start is not demanded; not even divorce is necessitated in the situation of adultery: there is grace for reconciliation even there, and I have seen that happen. That kind of reconciliation is a wonderful mirror of God's reconciling love for humanity for those who have broken their marriage covenant with Him. It requires great grace, deep forgiveness, but there *is* grace for forgiveness and reconciliation even in these situations. God can work wonders. But either way, even the tragedy and pain of gross sexual infidelity are not the end for a child of God. His grace is sufficient to give you contentment despite even great calamity (2 Cor 12:9-10).

Whatever your past, there is grace and hope

There is grace also for those who have come to faith in Christ despite all kinds of wrong relationships in the past, all kinds of breakdown, adultery, and mess, whatever it might be: grace to cover a multitude of sins.

We have seen that in these verses, Paul does treat Christians differently from non-Christians, as does the Lord Jesus; it is kingdom people who can live with kingdom holiness, not others. We cannot undo the past; the past is gone. Forgiveness does mean a real fresh start, and if you have been married and divorced and remarried before coming to faith in Christ, but have now come to the Lord Jesus, it is your marriage *now* that matters. You will want to seek to honour God in *that* with all your heart and your soul. You cannot rewrite the past.

Maybe you were divorced in the past before you were a Christian and you are still not remarried; what about you? That is more difficult to answer since it is not clear that Paul deals explicitly with that situation. Some think that the 'unmarried' Paul speaks to in 7:8, whom he says should marry if they are not exercising self-control, includes those divorced, but it is more likely he is speaking to single widowers 'and the widows'. Likewise, some argue that in 7:27 those who are 'free from a wife' means divorcees, but almost certainly he is talking there to those who are 'bound' in the sense of a betrothal agreement to marry someone (rather like engagement today, but with a strong legal commitment). But even if divorcees were in view, Paul says in verse 8 it is good for such to remain *unmarried*, and in verse 27 for those 'free from a wife' *not* to seek a wife – though he then concedes it is not a sin if they marry.

Though I do not think that we can find an explicit answer here, I do think that the implications of 7:12-16, as well as the general tenor of the teaching throughout the chapter, imply that Paul understands Christian conversion changes every situation. He acknowledges this will have implications for relationships, and that God has called us out of our past, however messy, and into His peace; it is now the present life of faith that counts. Where separation and divorce has happened before someone came to faith, then (however it happened) it involved an unbelieving partner separating, and so it is reasonable to apply Paul's verdict in verse 15: 'let it be so. In such cases the brother or sister is not enslaved'. That is in the past; they are a new creation in Christ, they are free to remarry as a believer – again of course, only in the Lord, certainly not to another unbeliever.

Nevertheless, Paul's teaching also urges caution in that situation. If you have been through a marriage rupture then the advice, 'do not seek a wife' and certainly 'do not seek a wife quickly', is wise advice. It is not a new spouse that you really need, to make your life what it should be, it is a new walk with the Lord Jesus Christ. The appointed time is short, says Paul. That is what really matters, that is the priority: the kingdom of the Lord Jesus Christ, which is eternal. Seek that first, to grow in His grace, and in the service of His kingdom, and all that you need will be added to you (Matt. 6:33). That is the real key to your life now, and always. We can trust the Lord Jesus on that.

Grace mends our mess

What about more complex situations, more messy relationships: like people who have been married and divorced and are now living with somebody else, perhaps living with somebody else's husband or wife? Well, as I said, mission exposes an awful lot of mess, and it creates all kinds of issues for the church. But, praise God that people are being lifted out of all kinds of mess into the light of the glorious kingdom of our Lord Jesus Christ, and into new and transformed life. And when people come to Christ, what happens is they recognise the mess, they acknowledge their sins, and they want to put it right. That is what it means to repent: we must turn away from the past, and we often must do a lot of clearing up of mess. Nor can we always sort everything out as cleanly as we would like. We cannot turn back the clock, and undo the past. Real repentance means coming to terms with that fact too: we must live with many consequences of things we cannot undo.

In practice, it is very rare that there is the realistic possibility of reconciliation with a former spouse just because someone is converted to Christ. They may well have had another partner for years, just as the newly converted person has. But to repent truly means no longer seeking to justify ourselves, but seeking to put right everything we can, moving out of the mess into God-honouring relationships. So the clear-up operation might mean having to regularise a divorce, and then become properly married to the current partner in a longstanding non-marriage relationship. But whatever it might be, there *is* grace for repentance, and there is grace for regeneration, for a new start.

And finally, there is also grace for restoration – for Christians who have made a mess long after they trusted Christ, for Christians who have sinned and acted wrongly and ended marriages wrongly. If that is you, if this chapter makes you feel very uncomfortable, then please hear this: the gospel is good news! The gospel is not just good advice or good morality. It is good news: there is restoring grace for *every* sin, and sin in this area of your life is not the unforgivable sin. There is no *cheap* grace in the gospel of Jesus: no room for presumption, or for self-justifying or loophole seeking. But there is *real* grace: grace for the penitent, the poor in spirit.

That is the grace and truth that we see in the Lord Jesus Christ. We have seen the fire of His passion, His clarity, His stern and rigid commands about the sanctity of marriage and about the real sin of even contemplating rupture of that marriage. And yet, it is also to Him we can come as broken sinners, pleading, as Bernard of Clairvaux's hymn expresses it so beautifully,

> *O hope of every contrite heart,*
> *O joy of all the meek,*
> *To those who fall, how kind thou art!*
> *How good to those who seek!*[5]

He knows our frame; He remembers that we are dust, and even in the calamity caused by our own sin, He is the one who will not break a bruised reed or snuff out a smouldering wick (Matt. 12:20). The Lord Jesus is the High Priest who is near us, and for us. And so we have hope. To the woman at the well with her five husbands and now living with a man not her husband, how gentle, how kind, how dignifying He was in His dealing with her, although absolutely true, convicting of her sin (John 4:7-45). With the woman taken in adultery, the same:

---

5   Bernard of Clairvaux, tr. Edward Caswall. 'Jesus the Very thought of thee'.

sheer grace to forgive, 'Neither do I condemn you', but also to impart that new life of holy living and of truthfulness and beauty: 'Go and sin no more' (John 8:11).

There is a fresh start, even for the fallen, shamed Christian believer; no, especially for the fallen believer: – If He can forgive His enemies, how much more those who are His friends, His children! Not for the self-justifying; He cannot do that. But for the sinner who repents, there is all the grace of the One who is the Saviour of the world. There *is* grace for restoration, for a new beginning, with our Lord Jesus; so surely also there must be grace for a new beginning among the Saviour's people. May God help us all in His church today to be such a people of grace and truth.

6. The Refusal, Removal & Renouncing of Marriage

We have been thinking all about marriage: the reason for marriage, the road to it, the relationship within the marriage bond, and about the very sad problem of marriage rupture. But of course, not all are married and not all will be married.

We saw in Matthew 19 that Jesus says clearly that some will be deprived of the sexual relationship of marriage for various reasons, either for a time or lifelong as He Himself was. Since marriage is a good gift of God, clearly not to be married involves a certain deprivation. The Bible is honest about that, and nowhere celebrates it as a blessing.

So it should be no surprise that many who live thus struggle at times, and sometimes struggle greatly, both with pain from unfulfilled desires, and with temptations which may at times be acute and hard to control. So I want to focus in this chapter particularly on those to whom marriage is refused, for whatever reason; or removed, either through bereavement or perhaps, sadly, divorce; as well as those who renounce marriage, as Jesus puts it, for the sake of the kingdom of God: God's call for them is to celibacy for whatever reason, whether their natural desire is for marriage or not, and indeed whether their struggle is therefore with natural sexual desire or due to homosexual temptation. Marriage is to be held in honour and supported by all in the church, even those who are not married. It is equally vital that those who know the blessings of marriage are likewise concerned to support those who, for whatever reason, do not.

A BIBLICAL ATTITUDE TO SINGLENESS IN THE CHURCH

First, I want to think about a biblical attitude to singleness in the church. Once again, 1 Corinthians 7 gives us some essential pointers. The key in this, as in most areas of life, is a right attitude.

> ... *each has his own grace-gift from God, one of one kind and one of another. To the unmarried [widowers?] and the widows I say that it is good for them to remain single, as I do. But if they are not exercising self-control, they should marry. For it is better to marry than to burn (1 Cor. 7:7-9, my translation).*

Singleness was once regarded as honourable, and not at all deprecated. But our society has so deified and idolised sex, that people are made to feel that not having sex must mean life is pitifully deficient. We have already seen that this is entirely false. The Bible rejects the idea that sex means fulfilment in life. Nor is sex required for a sense of belonging, or for the true intimacy of real friendship. Of course honourable singleness, living a chaste, celibate life instead of getting married, is very different from the kind of singleness popular today, where people avoid the commitment of marriage so that they can have serial sexual relationships. This 'biblical' singleness is not a deficiency, it is not a disease. Not at all; that is very clear from what Paul says here to the widows and the unmarried (which probably here means widowers), 'it is good for them to remain single, as I do.'

It seems likely that Paul himself was once married, as most Jewish rabbis were. But if so, he was no longer in that state, either because he himself had been widowed, or perhaps because, when he became a Christian and so dramatically changed his loyalties, his wife abandoned him due to the stigma of his faith. But Paul says here that being single can be good.

Of course he is not saying that celibacy is some kind of higher way of life, a more spiritual way of living. We have already seen how he urges the Corinthians to cherish marriage. Elsewhere he says clearly that people who teach against marriage and deny marriage are demonic, and very clearly commands young widows that they *should* marry and have children (1 Tim. 4:1-3; 5:14). But here in 1 Corinthians, as we have seen, he is dealing with a specific situation, a time of some 'distress', and he is saying that remaining single is perfectly good, and may be the wisest thing in such times. So singleness in itself is not necessarily a bad or harmful state to be in.

But not everyone, of course, manages singleness well, just as not everyone copes all that easily with marriage. Paul says that 'each has his own gift from God, one of one kind and one of another', so for many of these other widows and widowers, singleness was good, at least for that time. But he also says for some it was better to be married, 'for it is better to marry than to *burn*'. The ESV and NIV both mislead, I think, by adding 'with passion', as though Paul were talking simply about those struggling with strong passions, and his answer to that were simply to give up and get married.

But that would contradict what Paul (and the rest of the New Testament) constantly teaches about *not* giving up in the struggle for self-control over temptation. And, as any married person will tell, simply getting married does not bring the end of sexual temptation! No, Paul is speaking here to those previously married Christians who are already *in* another sexual relationship, but have not remarried. They, he says, must make it right: marry rather than 'burn' – probably meaning they should burn with shame now[1] because of the sin of living contrary to God's will (and perhaps also with the fear the burning fire

---

1   This is the meaning in 2 Cor. 11:29, where Paul says, 'who is weak...made to fall [into sin], and I do not *burn*' (ESV '*am not indignant*'). See John Richardson's helpful discussion of this passage in *God, Sex & Marriage* (St Matthias Press, 1998), pp. 31-36. I strongly recommend this excellent exposition of

of judgment to come he has already written about in 3:15). But at any rate, it is very plain that Paul is not saying that either singleness or marriage is a superior state spiritually.

I don't think Paul means that some people have a special 'gift of singleness' in the sense of relishing celibacy, or always enjoying being on their own, unlike other people who might find it hard and want instead to be married. Nor is he saying that some people have a 'gift' of marriage either, where marriage to them always seems a wonderful bed of roses, unlike others who find marriage quite a struggle. I have never yet met anybody who finds marriage a bed of roses all the time – at least, not thornless ones! No, he is saying something different, simply that the 'gift' that every one of us has, by God's grace, is the life and circumstances that God has given us at this time, and He wants us to be content and embrace *that* situation, not resist it. We often think that our lives would be so much happier and more fulfilled if only things were different: if only I had the situation that so-and-so had! If only I were married (or if only I were not married, or not to this spouse!). But no, says Paul, each has his own gift of God's grace. Each of us is called to trust God and serve Him in the circumstances God has given us, not circumstances that we might wish we were in.

That is the main message of the whole chapter of 1 Corinthians 7: '*let each person lead the life that the Lord has assigned to him and to which God has called him*' (7:17). What matters much more than any of our temporal circumstances, is our *eternal* calling, our calling to belong to His eternal kingdom.

Contentment in our calling

This explains a section of the chapter (17-24), which seems to intrude in Paul's discussion of these different situations of marriage, betrothal and singleness.

---

1 Corinthians 7 as one of the most helpful and practical brief books available in this area.

Only let each person lead the life that the Lord has assigned to him, and to which God has called him. This is my rule in all the churches. Was anyone at the time of his call already circumcised? Let him not seek to remove the marks of circumcision. Was anyone at the time of his call uncircumcised? Let him not seek circumcision. For neither circumcision counts for anything nor uncircumcision, but keeping the commandments of God. Each one should remain in the condition in which he was called. Were you a bondservant when called? Do not be concerned about it. (But if you can gain your freedom, avail yourself of the opportunity.) For he who was called in the Lord as a bondservant is a freedman of the Lord. Likewise he who was free when called is a bondservant of Christ. You were bought with a price; do not become bondservants of men. So, brothers, in whatever condition each was called, there let him remain with God' (1 Cor. 7:17-24).

This whole passage is about the contentment that comes from our true calling in Christ. What matters far more than your earthly calling, in terms of race or status or marriage, is your eternal calling in Christ. So do not be unduly worried about your particular status in life. 'Each one should remain in the condition in which he was called'. Maybe you are married; that is fine. Maybe you are single; that too is fine, you do not need to change it.

Paul is not saying that you can never change your life's situation; that is obvious from verse 21, 'Were you a bondservant when called? Do not be concerned about it,' he says, 'but if you can gain your freedom...' well, certainly 'avail yourself of the opportunity.' But do not think that achieving that change is the answer to all your needs in life; that is his point. It is plain that God calls people to Himself from all sorts of different life situations, those who are married, or widowed, and those who are single and celibate, just as He calls people from among the Jews and the gentiles, from slaves and free, and so on. And Paul says that seeking a 'better' situation in life, whatever that is for you, will not elevate your status in God's eyes: even seeking to be circumcised (or to become uncircumcised) counts for nothing. What counts is obedience to God's commands: that is 'God's will', what He wants for your life, whatever your situation is.[2] And just as circumcision or uncircumcision does not affect your status with God or in the church, neither does marriage or singleness.

So do not try and seek status with God or with other people by changing your situation in life, because your identity does not lie in your marriage status any more than it lies in your ethnic status or your work status. We must not be enslaved to other people's thinking about that. Paul reminds us 'you are bought with a price': you are precious to God as you are, so 'do not become the slaves of men' (v. 23, NIV), enslaved to the expectations of society or the culture around or indeed to other Christians who might think that a certain marital status, whether married or single, is something superior. No, if you can improve your situation in a way you would want to, like getting a better job, as he says to the slaves, or by getting married if you want to be married, and you can get married, then great, go ahead. But if not 'do not be concerned about it' for the wrong reasons (v. 21). Be content: there is nothing inferior about you as you are in God's eyes.

The Corinthian church was far too taken up with spiritual status, which is why in chapter 12 Paul is very insistent that the variety of grace-gifts God gives to different people are all for the good of the whole church family, and nothing to do with any individual's status. Likewise, whether married or single, 'each has the life that the Lord has assigned to him' and 'each is given the manifestation of the Spirit for the common good' (12:7). There should be no pride, no sense of superiority among any. Sometimes single people today *can* be made to feel somewhat marginalised and inferior in status in the church, especially if the church is largely made up of families. That should not be so. They must not feel that, and those who are married must be careful not to make them feel like that. Moreover, each of us is to be content in our own current gift of God's grace, because over all that

---

2   We have already noted Paul's emphasis on God's will for our lives being our holiness, in 1 Thessalonians 4:1-8 and 5:16-18.

towers our eternal calling in Christ. As Paul says elsewhere, in this life 'godliness with contentment is great gain'. (1 Tim. 6:6).

So singleness is just as honourable as marriage and, in some situations, it might be favourable, sparing people the additional burdens of family life in a time of crisis (as Paul points out in 7:32-35). In my own church are many brothers who have had to flee dangerous and hostile countries because of their faith, and those who are single are certainly much less burdened than those who are very worried about a wife and children they have been forced to leave behind meantime.

Singleness can also provide liberty for the service of Christ's kingdom where, in some spheres, having a wife and a family could make it very much harder. No doubt that was the case in Paul's own ministry, and many missionaries have likewise been enabled to serve Christ in difficult situations with their attention undivided by family concerns. I have single colleagues in our own church ministry who serve in tireless ways that simply would not be possible if they were married and had family. I thank God for them, as I do for two of my chief mentors in ministry, William Still and Dick Lucas, both single men whose unique ministries of such prodigious output and blessing to so many in the church of Christ the world over were surely, at least in part, made possible by their bachelorhood. Such a calling, for the sake of the Kingdom, is honourable indeed according to Scripture.

It is significant, though, that neither of these men ever suggested singleness as something others should aspire to for the sake of ministry, and indeed both urged marriage as by far the best way for most. They were exceptional men, with exceptional ministries, as was Paul. And Paul, too, is very careful not to undermine the blessing of marriage in any way, as the normal order of Creation. He extols it, and he protects it all the way through 1 Corinthians 7, because it is God's good gift. But what matters for everyone is seeing all this within the context of serving the kingdom of God, not serving yourself. God's call to His eternal kingdom must be our chief focus, always.

Detachment for our destiny

So, not only are we to have contentment from our true calling, we are also to live with a detachment from this world which derives from this true destiny that we are called to. Paul interjects another key passage into this discussion of the relative merits of singleness and marriage:

This is what I mean, brothers: the appointed time has grown very short. From now on, let those who have wives live as though they had none, and those who mourn as though they were not mourning, and those who rejoice as though they were not rejoicing, and those who buy as though they had no goods, and those who deal with the world as though they had no dealings with it. For the present form of this world is passing away. I want you to be free from anxieties (1 Cor. 7:29-32).

He does not mean for married people to pretend that they are not married, any more than he means that we are to pretend not to mourn when we are sad. He certainly does not mean for married people to ignore their spouses; he just means that we must keep *all* this life in proper perspective. In the light of our eternal destiny, what matters is not our devotion to mere earthly things, like marriage and sex, or property and anything else, but 'undivided devotion to the Lord' (7:35). Paul is not saying we are to become ascetics, or to abandon all these good gifts of God. But he is saying we are not to live as though *these* things are the permanent things in life. They are not. We need a perspective that sees what truly is permanent, not to immerse ourselves and our thoughts in the things which are passing away. Our true destiny is the everlasting kingdom of Christ, so that is where we must invest, with a healthy detachment from the treasures that moth and rust will destroy and thieves will steal. As Jesus Himself said, that is the only way to be really free from crushing anxiety in this life, whether married or single, rich or poor (Matt. 6:19-34). And Paul says that is his concern too: 'I want you to be free from anxieties'.

The key is in your attitude. Be content with your present calling, whether you are married or single, because your eyes and your heart are on your true calling in Christ which is everlasting. And be detached, not over-investing yourselves in the temporary blessings of this life that God has given you, because your eyes and your heart are taken up with that true destiny. Whatever our situation is, it is undivided devotion to the Lord that will liberate us from anxiety and from discontent. 'Seek first the kingdom of God and his righteousness, and all these things will be added to you' (Matt. 6:33). And so Paul says of his own life, whatever the earthly circumstances, 'I press on toward the goal for the prize of the upward call of God in Christ Jesus' (Phil. 3:14). This is how we need to think about both marriage and singleness. We need to have a biblical attitude that sees the bigger picture, so that whatever our state we too might live with both contentment and detachment in undivided devotion to the Lord.

A BIBLICAL ATTITUDE TO SEX IN THE CHURCH

Of course, all of us do face issues of sexual temptation, whether married or not, and we must be realistic about this. We need a properly biblical attitude to human sexuality in the church, not least in recognising the frustrations there may be for those who are unmarried.

Delayed weddings

There are a number of reasons why people are not married. For many today the issue is simply that of delay. They want to get married, they probably will get married, and may even have been going with somebody for a very long time – but they are not yet married. Often those in that situation struggle increasingly to remain pure. Well, if that is you, the answer is very straightforward: get married, and do it soon, especially if you are already burdened with guilt because you are in too deep sexually. 'If they cannot exercise self-control, they should marry' (1 Cor. 7:9). When passions are strong, 'let them marry – it is no sin' (7:36). He says the same in 1 Timothy 5:14 to young widows – get married.[3] Men, that means you need to step up, kneel down, pop the question and get on with it!

We need to confront seriously the unnecessary – and unbiblical – delays in marriage so common today; Paul says it is wrong, and harmful. Hindering youngsters from growing up to become adults is not good, and certainly Christian parents must not try and stop their children from growing up into adult responsibilities. If we think our kids are not mature enough by their early twenties to get married, then I am afraid that is an indictment on our upbringing of them. And we need to be realistic: if we expect a young couple to be together for years and years, or even to be engaged for years and not fall into sexual temptation, we are being naïve, but also cruel.

The church needs to take a firm stand, for one thing, against the worldliness of ridiculously expensive weddings, and the long engagements while people save and plan for them, which is one major reason why couples delay getting married. Often brides today (as well as the mothers of brides!) are determined to wait to have the fairy-tale wedding – yet ironically that can be to the detriment of what a wedding is really for, the marriage itself.

I heard a rare word of sense from a politician some time ago, when he quipped that there has never been a time when marriage has become so cheapened, but weddings so expensive. How true that is. But the church of Jesus Christ should be a pillar and buttress of truth, displaying the opposite: talking up the great value of marriage, but talking down the cost of weddings. If a couple should get married, we must discourage any impediment to that marriage.

---

3   In the Old Testament Law, too, the prescription for a relationship which had become sexual was for the couple to be properly married. Deuteronomy 22:28-29 gives this way forward, with the added proviso that a man married in these circumstances 'may not divorce [his wife] all his days.' The point is thus clearly made that with rewards of sexual relationship goes all the responsibility of marriage. A young man would thus be made to think very carefully on the consequences of his actions.

Difficulties, disappointment and disorder

But of course there are other situations. Not all can marry, or find a partner they want to marry. We have seen that Jesus Himself said sometimes there is a frailty, from birth or due to life's circumstances, perhaps physical or psychological or whatever it may be, which makes it very hard or impossible for someone to marry. Often, though, the disappointment just seems very hard to explain; I suspect we all know people about whom we wonder, 'why on earth have they never been married?' And of course there are those who are deprived of the sexual relationship they once did have, either through the death of their partner or perhaps, sadly, through divorce. I think it is harder for those who have had a fulfilling sexual relationship and have lost it, than for those who have never had one at all. And then of course there are those who are denied a sexual relationship because of disordered or disoriented sexuality, such as homosexuality, who know that their calling must therefore be to celibacy if they are to be obedient Christians. I want to say a little about these situations which, although different, share many similar difficulties. Perhaps none are more difficult today than unwanted same sex-attraction. These days not just the world all around but, sadly, even many in the professing church, want to normalise these feelings and to encourage their expression in sexual activity. That puts an intolerably difficult burden on those who want to live a godly life.

We must speak gospel truth

The first thing I want to say in matters of sexuality like this is that, as in everything, the church is called to hate sin. To truly love people means to be working and praying to help one another separate from our sin. Whatever our temptations, we are not helpless. The Bible tells us we are now children of light; we are called to walk in the light. We are called to keep in step with the Spirit of God who is within us, and matters of sexuality are just a part of that. They are certainly not the only area that matters when we talk about sin. But at the same time, avoiding God's commands and His promises for ongoing renewal is no help at all to godly discipleship in this whole aspect of life or any other.

We must face up to the biblical truth, which we may find very hard, and yet never underplay the grace and forgiveness, and the power of the gospel to bring new life. 'And such were some of you,' Paul says to these Corinthians, gross sexual sinners of all kinds, 'but you were washed, you were sanctified, you were justified in the name of the Lord Jesus Christ and by the Spirit of our God' (6:11). Radical change has taken place.

Listen to what one Christian saved out of a homosexual lifestyle has written about that:

We homosexuals who have repented and believed the good news have abandoned our futile, godless way of life. What is more, the miraculous has happened: we are 'in Christ' and having that status, we are new creatures: 'the old has gone, the new has come!' (2 Cor. 5:17). Something of the life of God has entered us, carrying with it far-reaching implications, not least in how we perceive and cope with our particular sexual tendency, and in how we relate to those in a similar situation... in all deliberations involving the homosexual question, one important fact must be borne in mind: certain brothers and sisters now seeking to walk in that newness of life and experiencing true freedom for the first time have been rescued from appalling homosexual degradation and very likely premature deaths. Some of them will undoubtedly carry deep psychological scars for a long time to come. Because of that, it causes many of us profound distress and hurt to witness the extraordinary spectacle of spiritual leaders charged with feeding or ruling the flock of God apparently encouraging same-sex practices, however sophisticated and refined those leaders appear to be. The last advice any of us redeemed homosexuals need to hear in our daily battles is that, in certain circumstances, the deeds that are 'natural' to us are permissible after all.[4]

---

4   Anon, 'One Homosexual's View', in Searle, D. (Ed), *Truth and Love* (Christian Focus Publications, 2006), pp. 67-68.

We must speak the truth. It is refraining from doing that which really *will* hurt those we want to love and support amid their same-sex temptations. We must not so fear being thought offensive that in fact we do actually offend against our brothers or sisters by failing them with our silence. In my own pastoral experience, it is those battling homosexual desires, more than any, who have encouraged me to teach the church the truth clearly, for it is the truth alone which sets us free.

We must speak gospel truth in love

But secondly, we must speak the truth in love; that is, we must exhibit the perfect balance and compassion of the Lord Jesus Himself. As I have said, no one's identity lies in their sexuality or their perceived sexuality. But many homosexual people feel, and they have been taught to feel by the culture and the media, that that is the case. So they feel that they cannot be accepted unless this aspect of their identity is accepted, even celebrated. So to hear people in the church talking about homosexuality in terms of sin makes them feel that we are rejecting them completely in their whole person, in their identity.

This means that as the church we must be very careful to exhibit that compassion of our Lord Jesus Christ. We must take great care in how we speak about these things. Sadly that has not always been the case. I want to quote to you from William Still, whose chapter 'Pastoral Perspectives on our Fallen Sexuality' in the book *Truth and Love* I commend as one of the most helpful things you could read. He was a man of thunderous truth, but also of tremendous compassion, as the many who shared their personal agonies and battles with him in this whole area of sexuality testify. He says this,

> We must return to the basic fact that God hates what is unnatural and nothing can make him change his mind about the abuse of the natural functions he has ordained for man as for his other creatures. That is the truth, this is where we must start, whoever we hurt...

...but I want to appeal for a new degree of understanding. I have in view those who, through no fault of their own, are afflicted with perverse desires and may be cruelly hounded to the point of suicide by misguided use of the name of God and Christ in the church. On their behalf, one must register a protest of complete condemnation of judgmentalism which utterly ignores the infinite understanding of the holy Jesus who, though he never excuses sin and must ever condemn it, always loves the sinner. 'Neither do I condemn you. Go and sin no more' shows the perfect balance of Christ's attitude towards all sin but with particular reference to sexual sin. In the interests of the compassion of Jesus Christ, there needs to be a far greater degree of understanding of why people do these things, however rightly disapproving we must be of their acts. Jesus' understanding of the woman of Samaria, the woman taken in adultery, and Zacchaeus, a very different case, shows us how sad it is that in biblical Christian and evangelical circles there can be so much harsh, cruel and ruthless dismissal of problem people. Too often, not the slightest attempt is made to understand why they behave as they do or to bring them to our blessed Lord's touchstone, 'Neither do I condemn thee. Go and sin no more.[5]

We need to take truth seriously, but we can speak no truth that will be heard, and received, without the compassion of our Lord Jesus Christ. How terrible it is that some struggling believer might be driven into the arms of those who will encourage them to sin with impunity, precisely because they have been crushed in the very church that ought to have given them a home. God forbid! Our biblical, evangelical fellowships must be places where people can find their true identity and their true belonging in Christ and among Christ's true people.

That sounds so obvious, yet it is not always so. Single people of all kinds often find it very difficult. Those of us whose gift in life is marriage and family have a real responsibility, to play our part, to give

---

5   Still, William, 'A Pastoral Perspective on the Problems of our Fallen Sexuality', in Searle, D. (Ed), *Truth and Love* (Christian Focus Publications, 2006), pp. 59-60.

the genuine opportunities for friendship, for family, for belonging, for intimacy, which all human beings need whatever their makeup.

Here are some more very helpful words from John Stott,

> *At the heart of the homosexual condition is a deep loneliness, the natural human hunger for mutual love, a search for identity and a longing for completeness. If homosexual people cannot find these things in the local church family, we have no business to go on using that expression. The alternative is not between the warm, physical relationship of homosexual intercourse and the pain of isolation in the cold, there is a third option, namely a Christian environment of love and understanding and acceptance and support.*[6]

He goes on to speak about the need to encourage widespread *friendships*, including same-sex ones, and to challenge society's suspicion of these, as if all such relationships were sexualised. No, as we argued in chapter 1, whether married or single what we need to battle loneliness is a healthy friendship culture in the church. If our hearts are closed to our brothers and sisters, especially those in real need, how can God's love really abide in us? asks the apostle John. 'Let us not love in word or talk but in deed and in truth' (1 John 3:17-18).

We must seek gospel transformation

Thirdly, therefore, as we think about a right attitude to living with our sexuality, we need to remember that the goal in all of this is the godly transformation of all our weaknesses. All our 'thorns in the flesh' (2 Cor. 12:7-10), of whatever nature, can be used as instruments of God's purpose by the grace of His power and by the power of His grace. Sometimes the very struggle and affliction that brings us near to despair may be the very means by which God's glory is to be displayed in our life, and the greatest blessing and fruitfulness for us also.

---

6   Stott, John, *Issues Facing Christians Today* (IVP, 2006), p. 476.

That is what Jesus said of the man born blind: it was that the power and the grace of God might be displayed in his life (John 9:3). Again, William Still expresses this with great personal insight:

I have known those who were faced with extreme temptation to unnatural sin who so resolutely refused to succumb to what fatally attracted them but which they knew was wrong, that I was astonished! But, on reflection, I knew why their aesthetic pastoral and preaching gifts were signally used of God. That very drive which could have ruined them was used when transmogrified into an instrument of God as the means of saving and blessing many. **But let me emphasise again that all such godly sublimation of seemingly innate sexual abnormality must be accepted and given over to God for death and transformation. This can be done only when the tendency has been recognised as a fault and a flaw and not as another kind of normality, it has therefore to be mortified, put to death, with a view to seeing how the Lord will re-channel its drive towards something to be used by God.** *It could then become as beautiful as the fruit of those to whom the gift of natural union is given. God has used people who endure agonisingly painful deviant tendencies but who have given their maladjustment to him for transformation. This is true of far more than many who are rigidly moralistic in the Christian world would believe. Some people hold up their hands in holy horror at even hearing that so-and-so has such a problem, but if they knew how sympathetic the Lord is to their affliction and how he stands ready to use it when we give it to him, they might be shocked out of their self-righteousness. Jesus is far more daring in what he does and whom he employs than many exceedingly pious souls dare to believe; that is why hypocrites do not like to get too near to him because He is a shocker.*[7]

If you find yourself living in agony with something of this kind, this can be true of you also. That is the message of the transforming gospel; God can, and often does, use our greatest thorns of affliction for great everlasting glory and fruitfulness in Christ. Ask the apostle

---

7   Still, pp. 62-63 (emphasis mine).

Paul; God's grace was sufficient for his terrible thorn, and abundantly fruitful through him. It is sufficient, and it will be fruitful with yours, if you bring it to Him, in submission to His yoke. 'My yoke is easy, and my burden is light' He says, 'and you will find rest for your souls' (Matt. 11:28-30).

Only bearing Jesus' yoke will bring contentment and fruitfulness if you are in a marriage relationship, and only Jesus and His yoke will give you contentment and fruitfulness without marriage. This is a biblical attitude to living with our sexuality. Otherwise, you will either be a miserable, unfruitful single person, or you will be a miserable, unfruitful married person.

A BIBLICAL ATTITUDE TO SIN IN THE CHURCH

But finally, I want to think about a biblical attitude to sin, and especially sexual sin in the church. Again, the nub of the issue is that we must show the balance of our Lord Jesus Christ, both His words and His actions. We must have no self-righteousness, and we are to show no wrong discrimination. But we do need the right kind of discrimination, to make the distinction the Lord Jesus and His gospel demands: between proud, defiant sinners and penitent, desolate sinners. The way we approach each must be very different indeed.

Proud sin must be resisted and opposed

Where there is proud and defiant sin, flagrant flouting of God's commands and refusal of His truth, we cannot pretend that God does not take that sin very seriously. We must warn those engaged in that sin, and if there is no repentance, we are to act accordingly. In 1 Corinthians 10 Paul uses various examples from the Old Testament to warn the church not to be sexually immoral as they were, or they too will face the same kind of judgments now, in this 'end of the ages' gospel era. He cites an example from Numbers 25, where there was flagrant, public sexual sin in the community and it led to fearful judgment.

The same thing had been going on in Corinth, and Paul's answer was very clear: where there is no repentance, 'purge the evil person from among you' (5:13). He is quoting the Old Testament law (e.g. Deut. 17:7, 12; 22:21, 22, 24) and saying to them that God still takes sexual sin among His people very seriously, and if it is proud and defiant, saying 'Look at us! We do not care. Look, God blesses all this!', then beware. Beware any such church, and any such people today, however much it professes to be Christian. You cannot partake of the table of the Lord if you sup with demons, which is what that defiant worship of sex is doing (1 Cor 10:21). In chapter 11 Paul reminds the Corinthians that some of them have been struck down with terrible illnesses and even died because of their sins.

That is a solemn warning to the church today. In the same way we need to take seriously what the risen Lord Jesus says to His churches in Revelation 2-3, where He promises that where there is pride and defiance in sin, He will bring judgment to that church. We cannot escape this biblical attitude, this Christ-like attitude to unrepentant sin if we are going to be truly Christian.

Penitent sinners must be restored

But very different is the penitent, desolate sinner – the one struggling in sin, seeking to be godly, but caught in temptation and sin which they hate and which often makes them despair. There, says the Bible, we must show great humility, and great sensitivity.

The tragedy is that some who have begun like that, hating their sin and struggling against their sin, have been turned into proud, impenitent sinners because of harsh and insensitive treatment meted out by moralistic, judgmental Christians. That is perhaps the greatest, and most shameful, heartbreak of all. No! Paul says. Those who are caught, who are trapped in sin, we are to restore in a spirit of gentleness, not a spirit of condemnation – all the while keeping watch on ourselves lest *we* fall into temptation (Gal. 6:1). What great realism: we *are* to go out on a limb, we are to take risks to help save people from their sin.

But we are not to be stupid, we are to be humble because we ourselves are not immune; it might very well have been *us* caught in that very sin, had God's grace not kept us, perhaps from the same powerfully seductive opportunity.

Do you ever give any thought to that, I wonder, before you judge somebody else? Or how often do we consider the immensity of the struggle that person might have endured, and how much they have in fact resisted before the fall which is so obvious to us? We might not have *any* idea of the deep loneliness, the misery, the hunger for love and acceptance that has driven them into that sin.

Robert Burns is not my favourite poet, and I certainly am not endorsing either his theology or personal morality. But his poem addressed to 'the unco guid' or the rigidly righteous does give a word in season here:

O ye who are sae guid yoursel'
Sae pious and sae holy,
Ye've nought to do but mark and tell
Your neibours' fauts and folly!
Whase life is like a weel-gaun mill,   (you, whose life is like a
Supplied wi' store o' water,   well-spinning mill)
The heaped happer's ebbing still,
An' still the clap plays clatter.   (clatter =idle chatter)

Hear me, ye venerable core,
As counsel for poor mortals
That frequent pass douce Wisdom's door   (douce =sober, grave)
For glaikit Folly's portals: (glaikit = daft)
I, for their thoughtless, careless sakes,
Would here propone defences –
Their donsie tricks, their black mistakes,   (donsie= stupid)
Their failings and mischances.

Ye see your state wi' theirs compared,
And shudder at the niffer;   (niffer = exchange)
But cast a moment's fair regard,
What makes the mighty differ;
Discount what scant occasion gave,
That purity ye pride in,
And (what's aft mair than a' the lave),   (a' the lave = all the rest)
Your better art o' hidin'.

Think, when your castigated pulse
Gies now and then a wallop!
What ragings must his veins convulse,
That still eternal gallop!
Wi' wind and tide fair i'your tail,
Right on ye scud your sea-way;
But in the teeth o' baith to sail,
It makes an unco lee-way   (unco leeway= great
                                                difference).

[...]

Ye high, exalted, virtuous dames,
Tied up in godly laces,
Before ye gie poor Frailty names,
Suppose a change o' cases;
A dear-lov'd lad, convenience snug,
A treach'rous inclination –
But let me whisper i'your lug,
Ye're aiblins nae temptation!   (you're maybe no temptation!)

Then gently scan your brother man,
Still gentler sister woman;
Tho' they may gang a kennin wrang,   (kennin = a bit)
To step aside is human:
One point must still be greatly dark –

The moving Why they do it,
And just as lamely can ye mark,
How far, perhaps, they rue it.

Who made the heart, 'tis He alone
Decidedly can try us;
He knows each chord, its various tone,
Each spring, its various bias.
Then at the balance let's be mute,
We never can adjust it;
What is done we partly may compute,
But know not what's resisted.

Robert Burns (1759-1796)

Do we see our situation exchanged with others, and 'suppose a change o' cases' before we rush to condemnation? Wouldn't we much more gently scan our fellow man or woman if we did – and if we considered that what is done, we only 'partly may compute'? We have no idea, do we, what someone has resisted?

A consultant psychiatrist friend of mine teaches regularly at the Pastors' Training Course run by Cornhill, Scotland.[8] During one discussion about dealing with very difficult personalities, he repeated something he said he had never forgotten hearing my father say years before, as minister of Holyrood Abbey Church in Edinburgh, where he had been a member. Somebody was loudly decrying another's behaviour, demanding that they be rebuked and condemned.

---

8   You might wonder why Psychiatry is part of a Pastors' training course, but not many experienced pastors will! Ministry is all about bringing people to the gospel and the gospel to people; so understanding people is vital. It is extremely helpful for those preparing for ministry to gain some insight from those who not just understand mental illness, but particularly disorders of personality, since such people can often present the biggest challenges in churches. Where expertise in psychiatry is combined with a clear Christian world view, so much the better. Glynn Harrison's very helpful book *A Better Story* is the fruit of just that combination.

Apparently my father just said quietly to the accuser, 'Well, try to think about how hard it must be for them; *and* just think how much worse they *would* be were the grace of God not at work in their life.'

I am very thankful that I had a father like that, and a pastor like that, who was, like Jesus, more full of grace than I of sin. I have often needed to ask myself, 'Am I a father like that? Am I a pastor like that? Am I a friend like that?'

Are you?

Grace humbles and gives hope

We can be so quick to see, and judge, what is done, but we often have no idea just how monumental the battles fought – and won – may have been before this fall, or how deep the grief and pain, the penitence and the shame, now. Nor do we know whether – in *their* place, faced with *their* struggles – we might ourselves have fallen even more gravely than ever they have. That was Jesus' challenge in John chapter 8 to those lifting up the stones, as we have already seen. He was not excusing sin; but He *was* saying: 'There, but by the grace of God, are you.' Suppose a change o' cases.

Which of us can stand tall in the realm of sexual purity – of body, of mind, of imagination – whatever our proclivities might be? And yet the Lord says to every one of us, 'My grace is sufficient for you and my strength is made perfect in your weakness.' So, humbled by grace, there *is* hope for all of us.

In our attitude to all in this whole area of sex, and sexual sin, we need to look hard into our own hearts, and we need to look long at the grace, the mercy, the kindness of our Lord Jesus Christ. Only then will we really cherish the truth in love one to another. Only then will we be Christians, and churches, loving not only in word and talk, but in deed and truth, ministering the powerfully transforming Spirit of the One who promises, 'Neither do I condemn you; go, and from now on sin no more'.

7. The Purpose of Parenthood

One of the first questions we ask after meeting someone for the first time is 'Do you have family?' For most people it is still a natural assumption that most married people will have children, or at least that they will want children.

At the same time, attitudes have changed and it is much more common today to hear people say things like, 'Are you planning to have children?' or 'I am not sure we *will* have children' or even 'Why would you ever *want* to have children?' (I know parents of young children do sometimes ask themselves that when their baby is giving them endless sleepless nights! Well, that does pass – though actually, they will give you different reasons for sleepless nights as they get older!)

In our society today, thinking about having children is much more diverse than the old assumption that parenting is part and parcel of marriage. The advent of contraception changed all of that, so much so that in many Western countries today the birth rate has dropped so far that governments offer cash incentives to have babies. Maternity pay, child benefit and so on have all increased in the UK, but this pales into insignificance when you look at other countries. Some years ago, Russia introduced a bonus of 9,000 dollars (US) if you had a child; in January 2007, Germany introduced incentives of 25,000 Euros for having a baby. For a while in Australia you got 5,000 dollars, but Singapore by far tops the list because apparently there is a total package of up to 166,000 dollars if you have and raise two children there.[1] You may be thinking you are living in the wrong country! But all of this reflects the fact that nowadays, whether you have children or not is much more a personal lifestyle choice than ever before.

And that means that Christians need to think very seriously about all these things. What is the Bible's purpose for parenthood?

Differing views in church and society

There have been different views in the professing church about family planning. The most obvious divide is between the traditional Roman Catholic position, which opposes all so-called artificial contraception, and the vast majority of Protestant churches, who do not. (Roman Catholics will allow so-called 'natural' methods, but that is a dubious distinction, because they are clearly artificially contrived for a specific purpose.) We cannot go into details about these things [2] but it is very important that, as Christians, we think about and understand the broader issues in a biblical way.

The Roman Catholic view stems from the thinking that the primary purpose of marriage is procreation, and that the relational aspect of sex is quite secondary to this. It is a little bit more nuanced than that, but here is the classic statement from the encyclical *Humanae Vitae* of Pope Pius VI in 1952. He says,

Marriage as a natural institution does not have as its first and innermost purpose the personal perfection of the spouses as in the will of Creator, but rather the awakening and rearing of new life.... other purposes' of sex, he says are 'essentially subordinate.[3]

---

1   See en.wikipedia.org/wiki/Baby_bonus.

2   Helmut Thielicke's book *The Ethics of Sex* (Cambridge, 1964), tr. James Doberstein, remains one of the most helpful sources for further reading in this whole area.

3   Quoted in Thielicke, p. 209.

Even if that were true, I would argue that it need not necessarily follow that contraception is wrong, but you can see how the Roman Catholic position on contraception fits with that view of the primary purpose of sex.

On the other hand, Protestant views, especially since the influential theologian Karl Barth, have more recently tended to be focused much more exclusively on the relationship of marriage itself as the purpose of sex, not procreation. Obviously that view sits much more easily with acceptance of contraception. If procreation is not primary, then of course sex need not always be for procreation.

The danger of this emphasis, though, which has become widespread in western liberal thinking, is that it can lead to a very privatised view of sexual relationships and a very self-focused, even utilitarian, view of procreation and parenting. That is the way our society tends to think today; it is your choice whether you will or will not have children. If you want to, you do; if not, if it is inconvenient to you – to your lifestyle, to your career, to your personality – you do not. And if you do want to have children then it is *when* you want to and it is *how* you want to. God really has nothing to do with your thinking. Having children is all about *your choice*: it is all about yourself, perhaps also your partner, but of course nowadays it is no longer necessary even to have a partner to have a child. That puts it baldly but that is essentially how our society thinks.

The problem for us as Christians is that we live in our society and breathe its air and, like passive smoking, we inhale much more than we ever realise. So we need to take some deep breaths of good, clean biblical air as we think through all these things in the light of God's revealed will and purpose for our lives. What is God's plan for our involvement in procreation and parenting? That is the question we need to ask first of all.

Biblical first principles

In asking it, we need to go right back to first principles in the Bible. Marriage itself, as we have already said, is for the purpose of glorifying God and of serving God's kingdom purpose in this world: that is, serving His sovereign purpose in Creation, and now in the redemption through which He is bringing His purpose to fulfilment through re-creation. And the Bible shows us that both the personal aspect of marriage, its *partnership* in life, and the *procreative* aspect of marriage, that is childbearing – *both* serve that one overarching purpose of God. (So too does the third 'P' of marriage, the *protective*, public order aspect of marriage: marriage as an institution. This is what protects the private intimacy of marriage and prevents sexual chaos in society.)

That third 'P' is a necessity in a fallen world, but the first two are integral to the very order of creation: partnership in the kingdom – man and woman working together as complementary helpers, and procreation for the kingdom – to fill the earth and have dominion over it for God. Neither of these tasks on its own is *the* primary task and goal of marriage; both *together* serve the primary goal of serving the glory of God's kingdom on earth. Nor can these tasks be separated. Remembering this helps our thinking in this whole area, not least when we come to think of things like contraception, because it lifts the question on to a higher plane than just one of biology, and whether methods used are 'natural' or 'unnatural'. No, we must begin our thinking by getting clear on the whole purpose of procreation and parenthood in serving the kingdom of Christ. That is how we will find clarity on the practical issues of both planning parenthood and practising parenthood, knowing how to raise our children.

So I want to focus on the purpose of parenthood as the Bible teaches us, and then deal with a few of the implications for planning parenthood which flow from that.

THE MISSIONARY PURPOSE OF PARENTHOOD

The purpose of parenthood, according to the Bible, is to bring to birth – and to obedient faith and fruitful service – the next generation who will continue serving God's kingdom purpose in creation, through redemption, until Christ comes to consummate that kingdom in glory. In short, we procreate and parent for the task of mission.

We must hold together parenting and procreation because for the Bible the latter entails the former. It is never just conception and birth in view; nurture in the faith of the one true God is integral to the true task of parenting for the Bible.

Procreation alone is not enough

Let us start at the beginning. The very first command to humanity is this: 'Be fruitful and multiply and fill the earth'. But to what purpose? It was to 'subdue it, and have dominion over... every living thing' (Gen. 1:28). In other words, to rule the world as God's representative, so that the whole world may glorify God in fulfilling His purpose in his wonderful kingdom. But, strikingly, even after the Fall and after God curses every aspect of human life – including childbearing – procreation is still very much to the fore.

Genesis 4 begins and ends with conception and birth (bringing tragedy with Cain and Abel, yet hope through Seth), and Genesis 5 lists the ensuing generations. God's purpose has not stopped, but things are far from right; the repeated refrain 'and he died' reminds us of the huge problem of death, due to man's rebellion against God. Procreation alone cannot now fulfil man's destiny to rule the world perfectly for God, because of man's sin. Now there are two seeds, two family lines: the seed of the woman, the promised line through whom ultimately God's source of salvation would come, but also another line, the seed of the serpent opposed to God's kingdom and His people. Genesis 6-9 charts the avalanche of sin that multiplies in the world as man multiplies and shows a humanity sunk so far from

His purpose for them that God must judge that whole human world in the Flood. Even afterwards, human evil just multiplies once more, necessitating the judgment at Babel. And so the message is very clear: merely multiplying the number of humans in the world will not save the world. There are more than 6 billion people in the world today and we are no closer to saving the world; in fact we seem a lot closer to destroying it.

Supernatural procreation is God's plan

That is why from Genesis 12 the Bible story focuses down on just one line, the family of Abraham, the line of promise, God's people of faith. They *will* be the answer to the world's problems because, after the Fall, natural reproduction is not enough to restore God's kingdom on earth; supernatural reproduction is required. It is procreation by faith, of the family of faith, that alone can bring God's kingdom to fruition and fulfilment – the bringing to birth, and to faith, of the heirs of God's covenant promise. In other words, missionary procreation. That was the calling of God's people after the Fall, and that is still the calling and purpose of Christian marriage: we mate for mission.

From the beginning the promise to Abraham was framed in those terms: 'I will make of you a great nation... so that you will be a blessing... in you all the families of the earth shall be blessed' (Gen. 12:2-3) – missionary procreation right from the start. This is what explains the great emphasis all through the Bible on fertility as a blessing from God, because it had a missionary purpose. So Isaiah 27:6 says, 'In days to come, Jacob shall take root, Israel shall blossom and put forth shoots [that is reproduction] and *fill the whole earth with fruit*.' Israel's fruitfulness is missional for the world.

So, for example, when Exodus 1-2 describes the Israelites multiplying and filling the land of Goshen, that tells us God is at work blessing His people for the sake of blessing the whole world; his plan of redemption is being carried out (despite the opposition of Pharaoh, who represents the Serpent's seed). By contrast, all through the Old

144

Testament, barrenness and sterility was a mark of God's curse, if His people were not fulfilling their purpose as a missionary people. Moses warned Israel from God that if she abandoned her calling 'cursed [would] be the fruit of your womb' (Deut. 28:18). That is not arbitrary, it is because Israel's whole purpose of procreation was bound up with the mission of God's kingdom in the world.

Supernatural parenting is God's command

This missionary purpose explains why the Bible is taken up not just with procreation, but with parenting. Bringing children to birth is never enough, they are to be nurtured in the faith and for kingdom service. The Bible never separates that natural side of procreation from the spiritual side. Parenting is never just natural for God's people, it is supernatural because it is a response of obedient faith to God's command and purpose.

I wonder if that is something you have thought about? We need to consider it carefully, because it is monumentally important for all Christian thinking about child-bearing and child-rearing. Having and rearing children is an act of faith. God never asks us just to have children, He commands us to nurture believing children, indeed missionary children. Of course God is sovereign and ultimately He alone calls to Himself those upon whom He has mercy. But at the same time, His sovereign command is that believing parents nurture their children in the way of trusting faith, and we as parents must respond to God's command either with faith or with unbelief, with obedience or with disobedience.

This is why the Bible has such a huge emphasis on nurturing in the faith, in believing homes within God's household of faith. God's promise to Abraham to bless his offspring and to bless the world through his offspring was a sovereign promise, yet at the same time, God made Abraham personally responsible for its stewardship. 'I have chosen him [Abraham] *that he might command his children and his household after him to keep the way of the Lord* by doing righteousness and justice, *so that the* LORD *may bring to Abraham what he has promised him'* (Gen. 18:19). God's promised Abraham a missionary family, and commanded Abraham, 'You must *nurture* a missionary family'. As for our father Abraham, so it is for all God's people of faith.

Deuteronomy chapter 6 is one very important example. After the giving of the law on Sinai, Moses expounds the life of believing holiness for God's people: how to live as His missionary nation Israel in the land that He has given them. 'This is the commandment – the statutes and the rules – that the LORD your God commanded me to teach you, that you may do them in the land which you are going over, to possess it, that you may fear the LORD your God, *you and your son and your son's son'* (Deut. 6:1-2). Never do you find in scripture the idea that we just leave our children to go their own way, to decide for themselves if they are going to follow the Lord's way. It is quite the reverse. God's command continues, 'You shall love the LORD your God with all your heart...and these words that I command you today shall be on your heart. *You shall teach them diligently to your children'* (Deut. 6:4-7).

God's people are to bring up their children in the nurture and admonition of the Lord. We do not ever find in scripture the idea that because God is sovereign we cannot do anything to lead our children to faith. God *is* sovereign, and so even bringing children into the world at all is a response of faith and trust in Him as the sovereign Lord, whom we know is good and just and merciful. (How else could we ever even think about bringing children into this world with its sin and curse?) So we must go on in faith and trust, obediently committing our growing children to God, teaching them to be sharers in all God's marvellous promises and His grace.

Godly nurture is steeped in grace

When your son asks you in time to come, 'What is the meaning of the testimonies and the statutes and the rules that the LORD *our God has commanded you?' then you shall say to your son, 'We were Pharaoh's slaves in Egypt. And the LORD brought us out of Egypt with a mighty hand. And the Lord showed signs and wonders, great and grievous, against Egypt and Pharaoh and all his household, before our eyes. And he brought us out from there, that he might bring us in and give us the land that he swore to give to our fathers. And the LORD commanded us to do all these statutes, to fear the LORD our God, for our good always, that he might preserve us alive, as we are at this day. And it will be righteousness for us...' (Deut. 6:20-25).*

You can see immediately what this instruction in the faith is not to be: legalistic strictures and harsh, unforgiving moralism. It is the very opposite of that! This is so important. Some Christian parents' idea of 'covenant' upbringing can be dreadfully distorted, very long on catechism and chastisement but very short on cherishing and celebrating God's steadfast, covenant love. That will only lead children to rebel against the gospel and the Lord – though they are rebelling not against the true Lord, but a perverted parody which is all they have really known. I have seen that happen, ironically often among those who make a great deal of 'the doctrines of grace', but who have in practice turned grace into a legalistic bondage.

But that is not what this is; the Bible explicitly commanded not to do that: 'do not provoke your children to anger, but bring them up in the discipline and the instruction of the Lord' (Eph. 6:4). That is what Deuteronomy 6 is about. God's people are to teach their children God's commands: *His* ways, statutes and rules – yes of course. But see how clear Moses is here: we are to do it within the context of the wonderful, abundant grace and mercy of God – who has redeemed *us*, now, not just from Egypt but from the bondage of sin and death and hell, and promised us the surpassing righteousness of everlasting life with Him! We are to bring up our missionary children steeped in the *glories* of redemption and rejoicing in the *goal* of redemption, which is to live as God's own people for His glory and for His kingdom in this world. That is what believing parenting looks like in the Bible.

Fathers must take a lead

We are told in many places that fathers are to lead in this responsibility as leaders both in marriage and in the home; they are to lead in the missionary preparation of their children. That is why it is doubly tragic when there is no father around: not just for the detrimental effects, particularly on boys, of fatherless households, recognised today even by secular commentators, but because of this added biblical focus for fathers to lead in godliness. No doubt this is why the Bible enshrines such a special care and concern for the fatherless and for the widow, and the church ought to echo that care and concern, giving special help when there is no father in a church home, for whatever reason. That is not easy, of course, but it is a responsibility we owe to one another as brothers and sisters, and owe to God Himself.

It can be such a blessing to a single mother, particularly if she has a son (or sons), to have another family, and another father, getting close to share the burdens with her, and give a godly, masculine influence for good, offering regular hospitality perhaps and a family holiday with them, and so on. As children grow into the teens, it can be a great help too, again particularly for a teenage boy, to have particular attention from one or more slightly older Christian lads, to whom they can look up, and see as a role model.

But where fathers are physically present, we must be *spiritually* present in our homes as well. 'Fathers... bring them up in the discipline and instruction of the Lord' (Eph. 6:4). That is not a helpful suggestion; it is a command from Christ's apostle. If you are a father, or will be one day, you need to listen to that: and by prayer, precept and example, to step up and bear your responsibilities.

The truth is it is very easy to leave it to our wives. We are very lazy by nature as men – I know, I am one! And, men are also very good at 'tuning-out' to our wives when they challenge us about these things. So Christian men need to challenge one another, asking each other as men, as fathers, 'How is it going with your Christian leadership in the home?' This is just one reason why Christian men, and especially fathers, need to cultivate good male friendships, something which, as we noted in Chapter 1, is often not nearly as strong a feature in our churches as it should be. But children need Christian fathering, and fathers need to be encouraging one another, and holding one another to account, to be good Christian fathers.

A mother's role is also crucial

Of course, do not think that I am downplaying mothers. Absolutely not; indeed, the role of motherhood is highly dignified all through the Bible. One lovely example is that of Timothy, that great missionary leader who it seems had a non-Christian father and was nurtured by his mother and his grandmother (2 Tim. 1:5; 3:15). We are also told in 1 Timothy 2:15 that women 'will be saved through childbearing'.

Of course Paul is not saying that women will gain salvation just because they have children. What he is saying is that child rearing (the word means 'parenting', not just having a child) is itself a wonderfully dignified and glorious calling for a woman, and bears great fruit for the kingdom of God, because parenting is a response of faith; it is a missionary task. We must assert that very strongly, because there are many today who say what they were saying then in Timothy's situation in Ephesus, that motherhood on its own is somehow rather demeaning, and that if women really wanted fulfilment, it must be found elsewhere. But God's word says to us that is not so; the supernatural kingdom task of parenting, as mother to your children, *is* your road to salvation! Do not let anybody ever demean that, and do not let anything usurp it; nothing else is more important to God, whatever the world may say.

This does not mean that a Christian mother should not have paid work outside the home, confining herself *only* to looking after her children. The 'excellent wife' extolled in Proverbs 31 has, among her many attributes, that of being a contributor to the prosperity of the household through diligent hard work and shrewd business dealings, and the simple fact is that for many (perhaps the majority) of couples today, it is an economic necessity for both parents to contribute to the family income. However, I think that Paul's words here, and the emphasis of Scripture elsewhere, do mean that motherhood – as a calling in itself – should be the natural *priority* for women, so that career or other aspirations are fitted around the needs of child-rearing, and not the latter squeezed into the leftover fragments of time from the former. Many strident voices today tell women they can 'have it all', but the truth is that you cannot, and your children certainly can't have the love, drive and devotion which you invest wholly elsewhere. Most mothers instinctively know this, which is why, given the choice, part-time work is what they want when their children are growing up; though not all are so fortunate, and for some it can mean difficult and distressing choices. We should be slow to judge others, but at the same time ready and willing to help those with young children think through the issues biblically.

It is this vital task of parenting that also explains why the Bible is so insistent that marriage must take place within the family of faith. We are not to be unequally yoked with unbelievers (2 Cor. 6:14), because if missionary parenting is so important, it cannot be shared with a spouse who has no understanding of this. That is why Abraham insisted that Isaac's wife would not be found from among the pagans and Isaac, likewise, insisted that for Jacob. It is why, when you read through the books of Kings, we are always told whether each king's mother was an Israelite or a pagan. If she was an Israelite, it boded well; if she was a pagan, almost certainly the king would be an ungodly disaster.

Similarly, Proverbs tells the young man to seek a woman of character, because beauty without godliness is like a gold ring in a pig's snout (Prov. 11:22), but a woman who fears the Lord is to be praised (Prov. 31:30). Why? Because parenting, and marriage itself, is for mission; it has been ever since the Fall and it will be until Jesus comes again.

Believing parenting is still part of God's redemptive plan

Some may think that because today we are New Testament Christians, 'surely now it is just about evangelism, surely God's family grows through the proclamation of the gospel?' Of course it does (and in fact, it has done right from Genesis onwards, when many who were not related to Abraham joined his family, were circumcised and became Israelites along with him). But God's creation purpose has not stopped now that Christ the Redeemer has come: in fact it has gained pace.

For one obvious thing, people cannot be spiritually born unless they are first born physically! But just as the gospel came to the Jew first, and then to the whole gentile world, so it is the privileged joy of believers to share the blessings of the faith with their families, and even more so now in the New Covenant than in the old. 'The promise is for you and for your children and for all who are afar off', says Peter (Acts 2:39), and the promises that we now have in Christ are not lesser, but the even better promises of these latter days of God's fullness.

So child bearing and child rearing are still part of our supernatural kingdom work. It is a fact of history that, like Timothy, so many Christian leaders have arisen from among those who have been nurtured in the faith of the Lord Jesus Christ from their earliest days, taking in the milk of the gospel almost with their mother's milk. What a privilege it is to receive that blessing, and what a great privilege to give! Our parenting is of the essence of the kingdom-serving calling of marriage for God's people: bringing to birth, and to faith and faithful service the next generation of missionary servants of Christ, until He comes.

PLANNING FOR MISSIONARY PARENTING

Having said all this about the purpose of parenthood, let me turn briefly to some implications for our thinking about planning for parenthood. The first thing to recognise is that so-called family-planning clinics today are almost a total misnomer. Overwhelmingly, their work is not in helping people to plan their family but in helping people, almost always unmarried people, to ensure that they will not have a family: not planning *for* children but planning *against* children. If a pregnancy results from a sexual liaison, then it is seen not as a blessing but a curse, it is seen as a disaster and a failure.

This, of course, is because most sexual relationships today never intend children at all. Sex is for sex, sex is not just for a long-term relationship, certainly not just for marriage, and certainly not bound up with procreation. That is our society's view today. It is also the view of sex that lies behind the sex education policies promoted so vigorously in schools, and which many consider to have done far more harm than good; certainly the huge increase in venereal diseases like syphilis and gonorrhoea is alarming health officials today.[4] But that is light years away from the wonderful pattern of marriage and parenting that the Bible presents. So we need to say something about how we are to think rightly about these practical issues.

Planned non-parenthood

First of all, a word about what I will call deliberately planned non-parenthood. As already noted, it is more common today for some to make a lifestyle choice not to have children at all. Our world is so perverse that children are seen by some as a curse and not as a blessing, an expensive burden and intrusion into your life. In a self-centred world where relationships and sex are just there to serve *me*, or to serve *us* in our relationship – when we have often elevated that relationship to the level of our god – then why not? But as Christians who take

---

4   Not far off half a million cases of sexually transmitted infections were reported by Public Health England in 2018, with Syphilis alone up 148 percent in the last decade, to the highest levels since 1949. The Western world in general has seen a rise in STIs over the last 10 years, with similar spikes in syphilis and gonorrhea in Australia, and STIs hit a record high in the USA in 2016. (Source, reports on the BBC (https://www.bbc.co.uk/news/health-44368741, June 5, 2018) and CNN (https://edition.cnn.com/2018/06/06/health/england-syphilis-sti-increase-intl/index.html, June 6, 2018).

the Bible seriously, we could never think like that, because children according to the Bible are always a blessing. They are a gift from God, never a curse. It is childlessness, barrenness, that is a great deprivation and cause for grief. Moreover, if parenting is a missionary calling, then to be anti-parenting is to be anti-mission and anti-kingdom. So we must conclude that a marriage that is closed in principle to all hope of children is in rebellion against God's stated purpose for us.

The German theologian Helmut Thielicke says this: 'There can be no doubt that a wilful and permanent refusal to have children on principle constitutes a reduction of the purpose of marriage in the order of Creation, a sundering of what God has joined together, and therefore something that is not in accord with the proper will of God.'[5] I think that can be the only conclusion if we take Scripture seriously.

Now, let me quickly say that there may be exceptions to this where, in principle, a couple is open to the hope of family but where circumstances mean that it is an expression of godly wisdom to refrain from having children. Sometimes a health problem would make a pregnancy so dangerous as to be an unacceptable risk to a woman's life. I know some fine, godly Christians who have had to make that hard, and for them very sad, decision, having been warned strongly by doctors that their medical condition would make it very, very unwise to become pregnant. Others may carry a very severe genetic disease, or others maybe just get married when one partner is at an advanced age, and there are issues, and risks, involved with that. These sorts of situations are quite different, because such people very much agree in principle that parenting is desirable and good, and want it for themselves, but in their case, sadly it cannot be.

But, in essence, I think we must agree that deliberate non-parenthood seems contrary to God's plan and purpose for human marriage.

---

5   Thielicke, p. 206.

Planned parenthood

Well then, what about planned parenthood, what I would call *proper* family planning? This is very different from planned non-parenthood. But the question some believers ask is: can faithful Christians take into their own control the management of their own fertility? The Roman Catholic church essentially says no, you must leave it all to 'nature'. Some evangelical Christians feel similarly, and I have known couples in some turmoil over this. So what can we say? There are many things we could think about, but I want to make just two points here.

Procreative union is more than individual sex acts

First of all, the Roman Catholic view which forbids contraceptive use in managing fertility is essentially reductionist. It is problematic because it is bound up with notions of what is called 'natural law' which really have more to do with medieval philosophy than the teaching of the Bible. It says that every single act of sexual intercourse must be open to procreation, because you cannot separate the aim of personal union from the aim of procreation in the sexual act. But you do not need to think long before you realise this view is full of difficulty. For one thing, is it at all realistic to say that the aim of procreation is always equally uppermost in people's minds while they are in the midst of the heightened sexual arousal of having intercourse? That seems far-fetched (and, one wonders, perhaps the sort of thing only a Pope might imagine). But, more importantly, it reduces the whole relational and unifying aspect of sexual intimacy down to mere biology. It means that *individual sexual acts themselves* are the only things that matter and forgets the whole context of an ongoing chaste and exclusive sexual *relationship*. Surely it is possible to honour and value and hope for the blessing of children within a marriage, without needing every single sexual act to be open to procreation.

We are stewards of creation, not slaves of 'nature'

The second point is made very helpfully by Helmut Thielicke: there is an important distinction between what we might call 'the order of nature' and 'the order of creation'.[6] Some Christians worry, about 'interfering with nature' by using contraception. Should we not just trust God? But God created man as a distinct creature within His Creation, not under nature, to be controlled by nature, but to have dominion *over* nature, and to be the controller of nature under God's commands and rules.

Since the Fall, this involves working against the curse that has put God's good world in bondage to decay. So you do not get up in the morning and say to yourself, 'Shall I put clothes on today before I go to work, or shall I just leave it to nature?' If you do, you will probably be arrested before you get to work, and rightly so. Or when you cut your leg, do you say to yourself, 'Shall I leave this to nature (or to God's providence?)' No, you put a bandage on your leg. The same goes for all of life, including planning and managing fertility. Thielicke says,

> *'Letting things go as they come' would not be the responding and responsible attitude appropriate to the claim of the order of creation, but only 'a bondage to nature camouflaged by religion.'*[7]

That is true. As we seek to be responsible stewards of creation and to live serving the kingdom of God in all things, including parenting, there is nothing necessarily wrong with planning our families and doing so responsibly. Indeed, in a fallen world there are so many factors that make life more complicated than we would like, and so planning requires a lot of real wisdom.

---

6   Thielicke, p. 209.
7   Thielicke, p. 210.

Planning and parenting that seeks the Kingdom of God

We need not fear planning families, provided that we are driven by godly and right attitudes to serve the kingdom of Christ, just as in every other aspect of our life: not just to serve our own selfish desires and our own comfort. We do need to challenge ourselves about that. Is our use of contraception godly, or is it just selfish? Both attitudes are possible, aren't they, even for Christians? And we must probe our hearts, because our motives matter greatly, and whatever derives not from faith, to serve God, is sin (Rom. 14:23).

But if we are seeking first the kingdom of God and His righteousness, then we are given liberty to steward wisely the task of parenting. There is nothing wrong with planning the *size* of your family as far as you can – provided you are open to God surprising you (and He sometimes does surprise you!) Some people can cope with having lots of children, and they want to; others just cannot, for all kinds of reasons. It might be irresponsible for them to have a large family, and it is not wrong to plan – provided, again, that decisions are made in faith, seeing children as God's blessing, not out of selfishness, out of self-serving.

Nor is there anything wrong, I think, in planning the *timing* of parenthood – again as long as it is a matter of faith and godliness and the worship of God, not of unbelief and ungodliness and the selfish worship of yourself. Each of these attitudes is possible, so we must be honest with ourselves, because God sees our hearts. One couple might desperately want lots and lots of kids, and want them straightaway after marriage. There is nothing wrong in that, but they still need to ask themselves, 'Is this wise just now?' Maybe they are still students, have no money at all, and they must pass exams which, if they do not pass, they will not be able to get a job and support a family. If that is the case, perhaps the wise thing to do *is* to wait just a little while, until you can do it responsibly.

I have known Christians who, being firm believers in letting God's providence take its course, shrugged off such considerations, had a baby before they were able to support themselves adequately, only for others in their church (and non-Christian parents) to have to bail them out financially to keep the family afloat. I do not think that is evidence of godliness, nor a good witness. A little more attention to Paul's words in 1 Thessalonians 4:11b-12 would have been helpful there!

On the other hand, another couple might be putting off children for years and years – which is probably much more common today. They need to ask, Why? 'Do we really need all this time: to get used to marriage, to accrue money to support a family, to be "financially secure" and so on? Is my attitude really godly, or is it just selfish?' Perhaps you are not seeing parenting as the blessing and the responsibility that God wants you to have; maybe you are much more affected by our worldly culture than you think. It is common today to hear people saying what many women are encouraged to say, 'I want time for *me*, I want time for my career, I want time for all these other things and then – later, when I have done all these things – then I'll have babies.' But the trouble is that later, you often will discover that it may not be nearly so easy as you would like it to be.

All these things need careful, godly thinking. We need to give serious consideration to the Bible's view of what parenting is for; it is for the glory of the kingdom of God, and that purpose must guide both our practice of parenthood and our planning of parenthood. Christian parenting is a missionary task: we seek to bring to birth, to nurture in faith, in order to bring to fruitful service within the kingdom of God. That is the way of faith for Christian family life.

So let us rejoice in that, and in the church encourage one another in this task whether we are parents or not, so that our churches are places where parenting is for the sake of the kingdom of God, and for the greater glory of our Lord Jesus Christ.

8. The Pursuit of Parenthood

Around 1 in 7 couples today face difficulty conceiving, approximately 3.5 million people in the UK.[1] The strain caused by this is therefore widespread and can involve deep distress, even, for some, inconsolable pain. A study of infertile couples done some years ago showed that 1 in 5 had contemplated suicide at some stage of waiting for fertility treatment. At least a third said that their relationship with their marriage partner was severely affected by the difficulty of conceiving, and fully 9 out of 10 had reported feelings of depression, isolation or frustration.[2]

Added to the misery of coming to terms with inability to conceive is the psychological and physical stress of medical investigations and, for many, undergoing fertility treatment. If it involves assisted conception, this may add considerable financial stress; the NHS provision is limited, private clinics are very expensive, and high failure rates often require repeated cycles of stress and expense. The price being paid by many couples is very high on many levels, and clearly this is a very significant, serious and painful human problem around us today.

Christian couples are also human; they feel all the stress and pain of infertility just the same. And perhaps for Christians it can be even

---

1   https://www.nhs.uk/conditions/infertility (Figures quoted as of 27 July 2018).

2   Wyatt, J., *Matters of Life and Death*, p. 75.

worse, just because we do understand the true, biblical pattern for marriage, and rejoice in procreation as an integral part of marriage, and a gift from God to serve His kingdom. In my experience that can compound the pain. So does the uncertainty many Christians feel over the ethical issues they find themselves having to wrestle with, as they contemplate possible avenues such as assisted conception. Over the years, I have known Christian friends, colleagues, family members and church members in this situation and I know something of the depth of anguish that they feel; I have wept for them and with them.

How are we as Christian disciples to deal with this whole question of the pursuit of parenthood when it seems to be frustrated, and indeed when it may be altogether impossible?

Infertility: a shared responsibility for the church

We have a responsibility to think through these things together as Christians for at least two reasons. First of all, many in our churches are struggling with this painful reality even now, as they find their natural ambition for a family frustrated. You may be among those, and if so, I want to try to help you consider some of the issues which will face you in a biblical way, because amid the very real anguish and pain of this situation, I know you want to walk worthily of the Lord Jesus, and not to grieve Him.

But secondly, and this is equally important, I want to help everyone to know how we can be real friends, real brothers and sisters in Christ, who can encourage and help those facing these particular trials, either now or in the future. We are called to bear one another's burdens, but the truth is that sometimes we not only fail to help, but even add to the pain because we have not thought through these things biblically. Unless we do that, we cannot be as supporting, caring and helpful as we want to be, and need to be, if our churches are to be true fellowships of the Lord Jesus. So, do not think 'This chapter doesn't really apply to me'; just remember that if it affects your brothers and your sisters in the Lord Jesus, then it is your concern. We are indeed our brothers' keepers.

I want us to focus here how we are to apply the Bible's teaching about marriage and family life to this whole painful area of involuntary childlessness. We saw that the increasingly prevalent idea of voluntary childlessness as a lifestyle choice cannot fit with Christian thinking, because God has made procreation an integral part of marriage, to serve His kingdom. But not only is that view wrong, for the couple longing to have their own children, and frustrated in their desire; that kind of attitude can be deeply wounding because it magnifies their own agony. When they would give anything to be able to have a child of their own, it is terribly hard to hear somebody treat the idea of having children in a derisory way.

This desire for the pursuit of parenting is a right desire that God has given us. But we must also ask how the Bible guides us in how to think when that desire is being frustrated, or even ultimately denied. First we must consider what is a proper godly ambition for parenthood, and this will help guide our thinking about the right (and wrong) ways Christians may pursue the parenthood that they long for – the godly achievement of parenthood.

We cannot be exhaustive here; nor do I want to be too specific or too prescriptive. We must be very careful about that, particularly when dealing with such sensitive matters and where ethical dilemmas can be complex; there are often grey areas where excessive dogmatism is both unwise and unwarranted. But the Bible does give definite pointers to sufficiently shape our whole thinking and approach on this issue, as in every area of our lives. Doing so, seriously, is part of the renewing of our minds which is necessary if we are going to offer God true worship in body and in soul, in lives that honour Him in everything we think and everything we do (Rom. 12:1-2).[3]

---

3   Truly *spiritual worship*, according to the Bible, is offered when our thoughts, words and deeds are 'not... conformed to this world, but... transformed by the renewal of your mind, that by testing you may discern what is the will of God,

GODLY AMBITION FOR PARENTHOOD

First, then, the Christian couple's godly ambition for parenthood. There can be no doubt about the very real pain felt by couples who find themselves unable to have children. Even the terminology can be very painful – infertility, infertile couples – and can smack of stigma, even of disease. And that is so very difficult, especially when the individuals involved are usually young and fit and healthy people in every other way. And, as I have said, perhaps for Christians it is even worse, because they understand the biblical teaching about children as a blessing from the Lord, and cannot see babies just as a lifestyle choice. So they may find God's apparent denial of that good gift to them a very hard thing to come to terms with. This is one of the reasons why our theology of marriage must be truly biblical, not just partially biblical; it has a vital bearing on this whole area of parenting.

Errors in different directions

If, for example, you take the position of Roman Catholicism that sees *the* primary purpose of marriage as procreation, it leads you to some very difficult conclusions about childless marriage. I quoted previously the statement from Pope Pius VI, that the *innermost purpose* of marriage *is* the awakening and rearing of new life. But if that really is so, then as Helmut Thielicke points out, 'the proper conclusion would be that a childless marriage is *not* a marriage, because it has *failed of its foremost purpose*.' He goes on to point out that this brings the Roman Catholic position into what he calls 'the dubious proximity to, of all people, Bertrand Russell' the atheist philosopher. Russell said very plainly that a childless marriage was non-marriage, it was of no importance to society, and it was 'unworthy to be taken cognisance of by a legal institution.'[4] He calls this view a 'rational ethic'.

---

what is good and acceptable and perfect' (Rom. 12:1-2). In thinking through these issues then, we are worshipping God truly.

4   Thielicke, p. 209, italics mine.

It is important to see the unpleasant places atheist philosophy takes you. That is not only deeply hurtful, but a terrible insult to everyone whose marriage has 'failed' by these criteria. But we must be careful to avoid going to the other extreme, treating procreation as if it hardly matters in marriage, so that only the marriage partnership and relationship define marriage's true purpose. Then once again having children becomes just a lifestyle choice. Perhaps something of that thinking seems to be expressed in Elkanah's response to Hannah, in her distress about her childlessness. *You have got me,* he said to her. *What does it matter if you do not have any children?* 'Am I not more to you than ten sons?' (1 Sam. 1:8) I doubt that was a great comfort to Hannah, or would be to any childless woman. No doubt Elkanah's motives were good, and we can understand this approach. Sometimes people feel, 'If we downplay the blessing of children as a good thing, that will help our friends who are childless because then they will say, "We haven't missed out on so much at all."' But that is quite wrong. Christopher Ash puts it very well when he says, 'To affirm the goodness of birth is not insensitive to those who cannot conceive or who suffer a miscarriage or a stillbirth, any more than affirming the goodness of marriage is insensitive to the widow. On the contrary, if we do not affirm this goodness we cannot grieve with them.'[5] Unless we do affirm the goodness, we are not dignifying their loss as something real and profound, which it truly is.

To downplay the desire for children is just as insensitive to the grief and pain felt by childless people, especially women, as it is to centralise procreation in a way that says your marriage is a failure if you do not have children. So, yes, we must be sensitive; but not silent. It is right to acknowledge the pain and the loss people experience and to weep with those who weep (Rom. 12:15).

---

5   Ash, Christopher, p. 181.

Practical answers flow from biblical truth

But we have seen that the Bible teaches neither procreation nor the loving partnership alone (nor indeed preservation of public order and decency) as the primary purpose of marriage. These are all the different 'goods' of marriage; but all serve *the* primary purpose of marriage, which is the service of God's kingdom through His purpose in creation and redemption. Can you see how important it is that we keep coming back to a clear biblical theology of marriage itself? There is nothing more practical in life than the Bible's theology – the Bible's view of life and the world. Only that will help us think clearly and find answers to all the difficult questions that we face in daily life.

Marriage is all about – indeed marriage was created for – the service of the kingdom of God. Children are a blessing, a gift belonging to God's plan for marriage, but because children are not *the* primary purpose of marriage, the bestowal of this gift in every particular case cannot be essential to true marriage, or to a truly fulfilling marriage under God's good and sovereign hand. We must assert that very strongly. Just like marriage itself, children are a gift and not a right for every individual case. It is normal to have children in marriage, in the sense of 'usual', but not 'universal'. We have seen how Jesus Himself says this clearly of the gift of marriage itself (Matt. 19:10-12); by implication, children are not a gift bestowed upon all, for various reasons – including the privilege of better serving the kingdom of heaven.

That can be desperately hard to bear. Yet, hard though it is, we need to remember that these words come to us from the lips of the Lord Jesus Christ, who was Himself unmarried and childless, for our sake, for the sake of the glory of the kingdom of God. These are the words of the Saviour we know and love, who in Himself He has given us all things and loved us with an everlasting love.

So if, like marriage itself, children are a gift and a blessing from God, then none of us can say that we have an absolute right to them. We are right to *seek* that gift, and we are right to value it, and have godly ambition to rear faithful missionary children for the kingdom. But if we rightly understand children as a gift and not as a right, this will shape our whole ambition for parenthood, including setting limits to the lengths to which we will be willing to go in order to achieve parenthood. We must think about that, because we live in an age when there are more possibilities than ever in history before to help us achieve parenthood when things are difficult.

GODLY ACHIEVEMENT OF PARENTHOOD

Even in the years since I was at medical school in the late 1980s there have been huge advances in the whole area of reproductive technology. Then, the first 'test tube baby', as she was then called, was still a young girl. Nowadays the science is no longer novel, but absolutely routine. But what are we to think about all of this as Christians? I want to give a very brief outline of the world's technology, the world's ethics and morality, and then seek a biblical perspective on these things.

The World's Technology

It is quite staggering what can be done in this field. Besides a host of drug and surgical treatments for different issues, more than eight million babies have now been born through 'in vitro fertilization' (IVF). Nobody today talks about test tube babies; IVF is a household term. It simply refers to 'assisted conception' by fertilizing an embryo from gametes (egg and sperm cells) outside the parent's body and then implanting them directly into the womb. Thereafter it is a normal pregnancy. The first choice for most couples is to use the gametes from the husband and the wife so that the baby is really theirs genetically, as well as having been carried by the mother. Of course, in many cases of infertility, that is not possible, and donor eggs or sperm are required.

In the United Kingdom, the whole procedure is governed by the Human Fertilisation and Embryology Authority (HFEA), although the role of that body is controversial, and many agitators in the scientific world want much more freedom to experiment, especially in terms of research on embryos. That is one of the problems in this whole area: currently established treatment is bound up with much wider ethical considerations. In Britain, there is a thriving Life Sciences Industry, with strong desires for further research using embryos, foetal stem cells, the whole area of cloning, inter-mitochondrial transfer and all kinds of new developments. The goal posts are always moving, and it can be hard not only to keep up, but very hard for us to know as Christians what we are to think.

Furthermore, IVF is not just a matter of egg and sperm donation now; there is embryo donation, from banks of frozen embryos which seem to be able to last almost indefinitely (although of course, only time will tell whether what may seem to be harmless now proves to be so in the long term).[6] There are also the headline cases we read about cloning, surrogacy and so on. Surrogacy, where in effect you rent somebody else's womb to carry a baby for you – whether you use your own genetic material or donated material or a mixture – is not illegal in the United Kingdom, though you are not allowed to advertise or to pay directly for it, so it cannot be commercial. It is therefore a very grey area legally, and there have been difficult, heart-rending court cases, where a surrogate mother has changed her mind and decided she wants to keep the baby she has carried, yet has been denied that, even after caring for the child for many months.[7] It becomes complicated

---

6   Potential long-term problems relating to reproductive techniques were flagged recently in rather sensationalist newspaper headlines which reported that people born through IVF were six times more likely to have 'dangerously high' blood pressure early in life. The findings were from a small observational study published in the *Journal of the American College of Cardiology,* and it is difficult to generalise from these data. Nevertheless it does serve to remind that, as an article on the NHS website discussing the study and its reporting put it, 'the technology has only been in use for around 40 years. So there is still a lot to learn.' https://www.nhs.uk/news/pregnancy-and-child/people-conceived-by-ivf-may-have-greater-risk-high-blood-pressure/ Last accessed 4 September, 2018.

7   In one recent case, a surrogate mother was forced by the courts to hand over the baby she had carried to a homosexual couple, one of whom had provided

not just emotionally and psychologically, but also very complicated legally, and recently senior judges have said that the courts are being put under severe pressure by the weight of these kind of cases.[8]

That just gives some sense of the huge minefield the technologies available today have opened up. But I want to stick to the much more limited area of a Christian couple thinking about how far they might make use of all this technology in order to achieve their godly ambition of parenthood; it is a question I am often asked.

The world certainly offers us a huge range of powerful and potentially helpful technology, but what is the morality of it all? What are the ethics involved?

The World's Ethics

The world's ethics tend largely to be about what we might call the 'Lego kit' approach; a term used by Professor John Wyatt, who is Emeritus Professor of Ethics and Perinatology at University College London (UCL) in his excellent book *Matters of Life and Death*, which is extremely useful in this area.[9]

There is no natural order to a box of Lego bricks: no specific purpose for the design; you make from it what you want – it is all facts and not values, if you like. There is no right or wrong way to use it, you just use it, you do what you can and you make what works.

---

the sperm for the embryo. The egg was not donated by the surrogate, but by a third party, Spanish donor, so she had no genetic link with the child she bore. Although in law the birth parents are the legal parents of the child, the judge ruled that the child, then 18 months old, should live with the homosexual parent and his partner. *Surrogate mother who changed her mind must hand baby to gay couple, court rules*, Daily Telegraph, 17 November 2017, https://www. telegraph.co.uk/news/2017/11/17/surrogate-mother-changed-mind-giving-baby-must-hand-child-gay/ Last accessed 13 December, 2018.

8   'Surrogacy and IVF cases put the courts under pressure, says senior judge', The Daily Telegraph, 28 November 2017.

9   Wyatt, John, *Matters of Life and Death* (IVP, 2009). I draw heavily on Wyatt's work in this next section, and strongly recommend it for further reading.

John Wyatt likens that to the view of many scientists today. To them, the human body is essentially value-free. We do not have to think about any moral questions: 'is this right?' We just must think about two things – 'does it work?' And 'is it safe'? This, too, is what governments are usually concerned with when making legislation. If it works safely, then it is good and we should have it. (You can see how this is the common approach to morality and ethics in so many ways in our society, not least the whole area of sexuality and gender.)

The Bible's Ethics

But what is the Bible's perspective? Certainly, it is very different. Of course, we are not told anything directly about IVF or these sorts of technologies in the Bible. That shows us why we must have joined-up thinking as Christians, in other words why we must understand theology, developing a Christian Mind.[10] We must understand the big principles of the Bible that are brought to bear on life so we can think clearly through such issues facing us today.

These big principles are very clear. A Christian mind, renewed and transformed by the gospel, does not approach these questions piecemeal. We are not just to ask, is this procedure right or is that one wrong? We must step back and ask much, much bigger and deeper questions. What does Scripture reveal to us about the whole nature and purpose of human life, and its purpose within God's plan of creation and redemption?

In other words, we need to understand what it means to be human beings. We need to understand what cherishing and guarding human life really is all about. That is vital in every area of Christian ethics. The whole Bible is clear that human beings are *not* just a Lego kit. We are not value-free. Reading Genesis 1-3 alone is enough to tell us that: God

---

10 I am glad that Oliver Barclay's excellent book, *Developing a Christian Mind* has been republished, since his plea for clear-thinking, biblically informed Christian thinking has never been more needed than in our ever more-complex world.

is the Creator and He has a definite design and purpose for us and this is reflected in our make-up as human beings, in body and spirit. We are God's masterpieces of design, we are made in His image, and for His purpose. All our thinking must take that seriously. But it also has to take seriously that the Bible teaches us we are *flawed* masterpieces.

Part of our responsibility as believers is to preserve and even help to restore the image of God in human beings. We are to protect, wherever we can, God's masterpieces from harm and to seek to restore human beings to their true selves, in line with God's creation plan. That is our rationale for preaching the gospel: we are seeking to bring eternal restoration of human beings; it is also the rationale for all Christian philanthropy, for medicine, for social care in Christ's name, for every good thing we seek to do to preserve and to restore God's image in human beings.

The Maker's intention is decisive

John Wyatt here uses an analogy that I find very helpful in thinking about this whole area of medical technology and especially reproductive technology: the analogy of art restoration, and the very clear and very precise ethics which are involved in that. He quotes from the *UK Institute of Conservation* guidelines:

> *Conservation is the means by which the original and true nature of an artistic object is maintained... That true nature is determined by evidence of its origins, its original constitution, the materials of which it is composed and the information which it may embody as to the **maker's intention**.*[11]

The maker's intention is decisive in art restoration. The restorer of a painting, or any object of art, can use all kinds of technology, all kinds of tests, all sorts of materials – but they are only free to operate within the parameters of the maker's original intention. In other words, it is not just the invasiveness of the technology, or its efficacy, which is decisive, but the goal: protecting the original intention of the maker,

---

11   Wyatt, p. 99 (emphasis mine).

not the restorer's view of how it should have been, or how it might be improved.

This point is extremely helpful for us, and can be applied to the whole area of reproductive technology, including those where a particular technique in itself might not be problematic, because the question is not just, does it work or is it safe? But does it use technology to allow the Maker's intention to be fulfilled? Or is it in fact changing the fundamental design of the Creator at a very deep level?

John Wyatt applies this to the whole realm of reproduction.[12] He makes the point that in God's design, making love and making babies belong together. DNA is the means by which the unique love between a man and woman is converted physically into a baby, into a new life. It enshrines in a new life the unique combination of love between a mother and a father. Indeed, each of our unique individual genetic make-ups chart a map of love going back over generations and generations. Contrast this wonderfully poignant way to express who we are to the outlook of many evolutionary biologists like Richard Dawkins, for whom the place of sex remains a mystery. They cannot really work out why it is there in the whole evolutionary process, other than just a way of randomly mixing genes in the relentlessly indifferent chance river of life in which DNA neither knows nor cares, but just is. But for the believer, for the Christian, sex is a way that *love* becomes incarnate in a uniquely cherished expression of that love. This is a very graphic way in which we can see that the personally uniting and the procreative aspects of sex belong together.

A real risk of reproductive technology is that all of that is left behind. Instead of God's unique gift of that incarnation of shared love, as Wyatt says, 'the danger of reproductive technology is that it subtly reflects and contributes to a change in our relationship to our own children. They become just a product of our will, a commodity at our disposal.'[13]

---

12   Wyatt, pp. 97-106.
13   Wyatt, p. 102.

Changing the Maker's design

So when we think about reproductive technology, we need to ask: is what we are doing allowing the Maker's intention to be fulfilled? Or, is it changing God's design at a fundamental level?

I think that if we look at it like that, then some things – which may 'work' and may be 'safe' – are clearly seen to be changing that design. For instance, as you start to think about egg or sperm or embryo donation, or surrogacy, or especially things like cloning or bringing three, or even four 'parents' into the whole equation of producing an embryo, at the very least you start to raise very big questions. You are introducing a lot of ambiguity about the child's identity and parenthood.

Some people may argue 'what really is the difference between that and a blood donation or a kidney donation?' Well, these kinds of 'donations' are seeking to preserve the order of creation, and to bring restoration and repair God's normal design: the *original and true nature* of the Maker is being honoured and respected. That is very different to introducing fundamental changes to the whole relationship between children and parents. This is even more obviously true where you have a single woman who wants to have a baby, yet has no intention of having a partner. With available technology, she can have a baby for herself, denying the child the possibility of a father at all.

Similarly, a lesbian couple, or two men who want to have a baby today can achieve this through IVF donation and surrogacy. The degree to which such things are now becoming 'normal' is surely clear when (at the time of writing) the leader of the Conservative Party in Scotland is pregnant with her same-sex partner, and this seems only to have increased the odds on her becoming a future Conservative Prime Minister. But however common, and increasingly acceptable, this kind of situation may now be in our society, as Christians we must firmly insist that the Maker's original design is decisive, and here efforts are being made to change and counter that proper order.

Restoring the Maker's intention?

What about standard IVF using gametes from both parents? Can Christian parents in good conscience seek assisted conception using this kind of technology?

My own conclusion, having wrestled with the issue from both a medical and theological perspective over the years, is yes: that this can be regarded as a restorative technology, enabling a couple to achieve what some particular problem or 'blockage in the system' in their case is simply preventing – an incarnation of their own love in a child who is their own.[14]

I say this is my personal view, with which others may feel uncomfortable for themselves, and I would never want to encourage any who felt that way to embark upon something they felt was wrong. Paul's discussion in Romans 14 is very pertinent in this area; we must not make others stumble, nor act in ways we ourselves cannot pursue in faith and good conscience. And, the answer is never quite so simple in practice. I would enter several caveats which are very important.

One is that no excess embryos are created simply for destruction or for research purposes. We must take the formation of human life like that very seriously. In the past, because they were seeking the highest possible success rates, many clinics insisted on creating multiple embryos, almost guaranteeing embryo wastage, and also implanting multiple embryos into the womb, sometimes then with selective destruction (early abortion) of some to avoid the risks of multiple pregnancies. More recently, however, success rates are such that clinics seem more willing to accommodate the desire to create only the minimum number of embryos required, and Christians (as well as others) have been able to have successful treatment without creating 'spare' embryos.

Another caveat is that, despite this, we must admit that a lot of the technology which now makes this routine has been developed through

14   This is also the view John Wyatt expresses in *Matters of Life and Death*, pp. 103-104.

research in the past which did result in the destruction of countless thousands of embryos; we cannot escape from the reality that we are benefitting today from the fruit of such actions. Of course that is equally true for many medical procedures, drugs, and all sorts of things we benefit from today, but which likewise have been created through research that we might find repulsive. But for some, the knowledge of this will make IVF something they may find too troubling to contemplate.

A third important thing to consider, and which I always emphasise when I am counselling couples, is that IVF is certainly not without risk, and can be very stressful indeed. Remember the statistics at the beginning of the chapter. Going down this road is physically demanding, emotionally very draining, and often causes very serious strain on one, if not both partners in a marriage, and to the marriage itself. I know that through sharing in the experience of others (both Christians and non-Christian friends). Very careful thought is needed before you embark on it. I know couples who have thought long and hard about all the issues involved, and, despite concluding (as I do) that it is not a *wrong* road for them, for these and other reasons, have realised it is just not the *wisest* road for them, and for their marriage, and so have decided not to pursue it further.

My advice to you if you are thinking of going down this route, is that you read further and research these things so that you really *know the issues* involved. John Wyatt's book, *Matters of Life and Death,* is an excellent place to start.[15] But you also need to *know yourself,* and your spouse, and be realistic about whether what is involved really is what you want to pursue. Close friends, and – hopefully – a sensitive and understanding pastor who knows you, will be able to help you think and talk these things through, and pray with you as you seek God's wisdom for this most difficult of decisions in life.

---

15   Wyatt, John, *Matters of Life and Death* (IVP, 2009). This book also contains a list of other useful resources. The Christian Medical Fellowship (www.cmf.org.uk) also has a lot of helpful literature.

This is just a sketch of the key issues involved in the consideration of assisted reproduction, but I hope it will help just to guide your further thinking in this difficult area. But in drawing some conclusions, I want to restate the basic question: how far should godly parents go in pursuing parenthood?

Achieving the ambition of parenting

That is going to be determined fundamentally by how much we see it as a gift from God and how much we see parenthood as a right that we can demand. It is good and right to have the ambition for parenthood, so I think it would be foolish not to pursue, for example, basic medical tests and treatment, because lots of things can help to restore the masterpiece of the Maker's intent. Some Christians can be very slow to seek 'secular' help for something they feel is a matter of God's sovereignty. But that is mistaken; God's common grace has blessed all humanity with medical science, so how much more does He bless His precious children with these things. So do not be slow to seek help from your GP as a first port of call. Some issues may be quite simple, and relatively easy to treat.

But at the same time, we also must say that our ambition to pursue parenthood cannot be unlimited, because we do recognise that it is a gift, not a right for every marriage. Those limits might be due to ethical issues, or simply just due to practicalities and wisdom: the sheer exhaustion and stress of the treadmill of endless investigations and treatment. Not everything that is permissible to us as Christians is wise for all Christians in their circumstances. We must be real about that.

Adoption

What other options are there? Of course, one very honourable tradition is that of adoption. From very earliest times, Christians were renowned for rescuing orphans and foundlings, and later were the pioneers of care homes, adoption services, and fostering. But one of the great tragedies of the huge expansion of abortion is that there are so many fewer babies for adoption than in the past. In the thirty years that followed the UK Abortion Act in 1967, the number of babies being adopted in this country was reduced to less than a quarter of what it had been.[16] But adoption is certainly still one option for Christian would-be parents.

Yet even in this area, noble as it is, we still must ask the question, why? Just as in planning to have children any other way, naturally, or through infertility treatments, you need to ask: is it just for me? Is it for our desire to achieve *a child at all costs*? Or, is our attitude deeply suffused also by a desire to serve the kingdom of God? Some very 'pious' Christians thoroughly disapprove of any sort of reproductive technology (and often of those who go through such procedures), yet they themselves have gone – literally – to the very ends of the earth to adopt exactly the perfect kind of baby that they want to have, because they do not want the children on offer for adoption here. No doubt it is a natural desire, if considering adoption, to want a baby, and not perhaps an older child. But, just as with all God's gifts, we must submit our desires to Him. What kind of child will I accept if we are going to adopt? Must it be the perfect baby?

Even when we conceive children by ordinary means, God does not always give us a perfect baby; sometimes it is a baby with grave problems or handicaps. And parenting is not just for us, and our satisfaction, it is for God; it is a response of obedient faith to Him, whether the child is our natural child, or an adopted child. It is God's gift for a purpose. True fulfilment is found in that purpose, not in our having the child that we want. We need to think about that, and to think about what our real motives are, whatever way we seek to achieve them, even if it is through adoption. Is it to serve God's kingdom in faith and fruitfulness?

You need to realise, too, that it might be a very tough assignment. Many of the children who come into families for adoption today, come from very difficult backgrounds, and can be terribly wounded, even at

16   Wyatt, p.148.

a very young and tender age. But this means adoption can be a very wonderful and glorious calling.

In my personal experience, it is rarely an easy calling, and it seems to me that adoptive parents often bear all the normal parental burdens, with many more besides. So like everything, you need to go into it with your eyes open and your hearts open to God's purpose and His plan. Then adoption can be a beautiful thing. Never forget that our heavenly Father is the great adopter – of the damaged, the difficult, the unlovely and unloved. This wonderful truth lies at the very heart of the gospel. So adoption is certainly a very honourable path for a Christian couple, provided they are realistic and their ambition is to serve God's purpose, and not just their own ambition for family.

Acceptance

But for others, the response may simply be acceptance. Some couples just come to the point where they accept that, for them, there are to be no children. That can mean bitterness and resentment, life lived with a great chip on your shoulder. But it need not be like that, if – despite the pain and the grief and the real sense of bereavement – they can see, and are helped to see, that even this situation can be captured for the glory of Christ. Then it can in fact lead to a wonderful, fruitful release to serve Christ in ways they could never have imagined, ways that would otherwise, with family, have been much harder, or even impossible altogether.

If childlessness, just like singleness or any other deprivation, can itself be seen as a gift from the Lord in these kingdom terms, a grace in life to be used for Him, then the freedom and the joy in that is enormous. Using it for Him can bring immense pleasure, and purpose, and great fulfilment in life – even though it is forged through years of great agony. I can think of those that I have known personally over the years for whom this has been wonderfully true in extraordinary ways. I think of one dear friend who, if anybody was ever made for motherhood, it was she. Yet, very painfully for her, children never came. But, in time, that opened up a path for Christian service in a way that was quite remarkable. I remember her once saying to me, with tears in her eyes, 'God has given me the joy of so many children I would never have had if I'd actually had my own ones.'

That was not without great pain. Yet in it there was great joy, real joyous fulfilment and blessing in serving the kingdom of the Lord. But that is, of course, the promise of our Lord Jesus. It is in Matthew 19, the very chapter where He talks about marriage, and children, that He tells us that no-one who has forgone precious relationships of love in this life for the sake of the Lord will ever lose out. He *will* compensate – a hundredfold, even now in this life, and in the world to come an inheritance of glorious life (Matt. 19:29).

Abiding hope

I want to end this chapter about godly ambition for parenthood with some words from Isaiah 56 which direct our hearts towards that *new* world the Lord Jesus constantly holds before us as the ultimate ambition for all of us who are His. They are words of wonderful comfort and hope for all whose hearts are wrenched by pain because of this issue, and indeed any of the other issues we have been thinking about throughout this book.

> *...soon my salvation will come, and my righteousness be revealed... Let not the foreigner who has joined himself to the LORD say, 'The LORD will surely separate me from his people'; and let not the eunuch say, 'Behold, I am a dry tree.' For thus says the LORD: 'To the eunuchs who keep my Sabbaths, who choose the things that please me and hold fast my covenant, I will give in my house and within my walls a monument and a name better than sons and daughters. I will give them an everlasting name that shall not be cut off'* (Isa. 56:1-5).

That is the promise of the gospel of our Lord Jesus Christ: the *great restoration to the Maker's true intention* for every single one who knows and loves Him. Whatever we may have lacked in this veil of tears, whatever unfilled desires there may be in our lives – this is what we long for, and wait for with confident joy, in Jesus our Saviour.

So may the Lord help us to help each other to do that: to hope for His glory, even through the tears and the grief and the pain there will be along the way. And may we, as Christ's precious people, be a people pointing to that hope, always.

9. A Final Word

*Father of the fatherless and protector of widows... God settles the solitary in a **home** (Ps. 68:5).*

*A man of many companions may come to ruin, but there is a **friend who sticks closer than a brother** (Prov. 18:24).*

*No longer do I call you servants, ... but I have called you **friends**, for all that I have heard from my Father I have made known to you (John 15:15).*

*I have loved you with an **everlasting love** (Jer. 31:3).*

*This is my commandment, that **you love one another as I have loved you**... You are my friends if you do what I command you (John 15:12, 14).*

We began by considering the wonderful truth about the Lord our God who delights to bestow friendship and love, family and real belonging upon His people. And in our Lord Jesus Christ, He who is 'father to the fatherless and protector of widows' came into our darkness, the loneliness and alienation of our sin, to rescue us and bring us truly home. In Him we all may know *the* friend – the one closer than the nearest kin, who brings all the secrets of the Father in heaven, and who loves us with an everlasting love. Only His friendship will never let us come to ruin; only his love will never disappoint, or fade away.

And only in a deep understanding of His love lies the answer to all the inconsolable longing for love deep within our hearts.

Moreover, only in a deep sharing in His love lies the answer to the way of loving others that will enrich and bless and satisfy them, and us, in every relationship we have in life. For it is *this* love – not envious, arrogant, insisting on its own way, not irritable or resentful, but patient, kind, rejoicing in truth, bearing all things, enduring all things – *His* love truly incarnate in us, which never ends (1 Cor. 13:4-8).

So, in every aspect of our love one to another, let us determine to love as He has loved us. When we do, we shall find it is this holy living, under His gracious commandment, which truly liberates for healthy loving, and for all the truly fruitful love our hearts crave.

Further Reading

C. S. Lewis, *The Four Loves* (Collins, 2012)

A must read, especially for the wonderful chapter on friendship. Readable and full of insight.

Christopher Ash, *Marriage: Sex in the Service of God* (IVP, 2016)

A substantial and detailed scholarly work, but for those who like a challenge this is the best book on marriage anywhere. See also his abbreviated book, *Married for God: Making Your Marriage the Best It Can Be* (IVP, 2007), which makes a great gift for those getting married.

John Murray, *Divorce* (P&R, 2012)

Another challenging book, but works through the key Bible passages carefully and accurately.

Frank Retief, *Divorce* (Christian Focus, 2010)

A very readable book applying the Biblical perspective to the many thorny issues surrounding divorce in a gracious pastoral way.

Glynn Harrison, *A Better Story: God, Sex and Human Flourishing* (IVP, 2017)

Another engaging read, which shows how contemporary attitudes on sex and sexuality fail to deliver what they promise – and how the church can show, instead, the goodness of God's view of sex and relationships.

David Searle (Ed), *Truth and Love* (Christian Focus, 2006)

A selection of essays by different authors on sex, morality and personal identity, some of which are invaluable – particularly those by William Still which I have quoted.

Helmut Thielicke, *The Ethics of Sex,* tr. James Doberstein, (Cambridge, 1964)

A serious but insightful book for pastors and others thinking hard about the ethics of marriage and sex.

Timothy Sizemore, *Of Such is the Kingdom: nurturing children in the light of Scripture* (Christian Focus, 2000)

A helpful practical book for Christian parents seeking to nurture children in faith.

John Wyatt, *Matters of Life and Death* (IVP 2009)

The key book for anyone thinking about issues of medical ethics, written by a senior doctor who is also a Professor of Ethics and Perinatology. It thinks carefully through difficult questions and case-studies with Biblical wisdom and real compassion.

John Frame, *The Doctrine of the Christian Life* (P&R, 2018)

An extraordinarily insightful book on Christian ethics, which deals with key issues on marriage and gender roles among many others. This is a major theological work, but very accessible.

See the footnotes for details of other books referenced.

Acknowledgments

I am grateful to many who have helped and encouraged in bringing this book to fruition. Dorothy Campbell, who produces transcripts from my preaching far faster than I can possibly process and work on them, has waited very patiently to see the fruit of her labours; I am immensely grateful for her tireless devotion to what would be, for most, a tedious task, but without which I should never have been able to begin this book. Sam Parkinson's editorial help has been invaluable, and I am particularly grateful for the many places where his gentle insistence on addition, subtraction or clarification of material has made the book far better, and more readable, than it would have otherwise been. My friend Simon Manchester, in suggesting and providing the 'think it through' questions, has given the book a valuable resource which will, I hope, add to its usefulness for group study or marriage preparation with couples. I am also very thankful to my friend and fellow-worker in the gospel, Richard Henry, whose quiet determination to see the material in print eventually wore me down and forced me to get to work.

Above all, I am grateful to the Lord for both my own family and our spiritual family of The Tron Church, whom I love deeply, and who have loved me with such patience and persistence over the years. I delight in the privilege we have of learning together from the unsearchable riches of Christ, and my chief desire and prayer is that the message of these pages may bring help, encouragement and hope to them, as well as others, in the generations to come.

Think it Through Discussion Questions
(For Use in Small Groups)

INTRODUCTION AND CHAPTER ONE – THE FOUNDATION OF FRIENDSHIP

1. (Intro) Try and identify whether members of the group have one friend (or more) who they could talk to about deep struggles or sins. As an option you could say who that person is.

2. In the introduction the author quotes 1 John 4:19 – that God 'loved' His people first. Do you believe that or feel it – and why?

3. What would help you or this group 'learn together' and not just stay the same?

4. In chapter one we are introduced to John 15. Read 15:9-17 and ask yourself what this love might have looked like in action as the first disciples took Jesus seriously.

5. What does 'loneliness' feel like? Why is there such loneliness when 'communication' is easily available? Do you agree that a common interest is crucial to friendship?

6. Which dangers raised by the author (gender-neutrality, marriage over-expectations, inward focusing) strike you as being particularly relevant to church today?

7. Have you experienced the Proverbs 17:17 type of friendship? Are you grateful for the Proverbs 27:6 person who has helped you? Mention examples briefly.

8. What steps might you take to stop waiting for a friend and start being a friend? Why can you be confident the Lord will bless this initiative?

CHAPTER TWO – THE REASON FOR MARRIAGE

1. (Intro) Make a brief list of the advantages in being single. Then of being married. Make a brief list of the challenge in being single. Then of being married. Do any of these 'good' options (1 Cor. 7:8-9) solve all our problems?

2. Do you think Christians know that their marriage is 'from God' and 'for God'? Do you suspect that many (even Christians) get married with God somewhere in the background?

3. The author points out that the 'weak' (the children, the poor) will suffer as marriages crumble – why is the glue of former days disappearing so fast?

4. So often the marriage services in church will seem to highlight companionship and children as priorities for a marriage – why is 'the furtherance of God's purpose in this world' such a biblical and proper corrective? And why is the message of 'redemption' (Matt. 28:18-20) so important for a couple to promote together?

5. What would it look like for a couple to 'partner' together in serving God's purpose for the world? Have you seen couples do this well?

6. A secular politician has to balance the cost of societal breakdown (as marriages fail) with the pressure of societal demands (to marry whoever people want to) – why would Mark 7:20-23 be a good dose of realism to help them protect marriage?

7. Imagine you received the Colossian letter. Why can Paul safely say so little (3:18-21) about marriage or family? [Clue: 1:1-3:17!]

8. Why does the gospel present us with such help for past mistakes, help for present struggles and hope for future joys?

CHAPTER THREE – THE ROAD TO MARRIAGE

1. This chapter wisely (and bravely) talks of the paths to marriage. In the past this was an exciting path to get on to – do you think this is still the case? What makes you think the way you do?

2. The comparison of sex to 'petrol' (good in context but dangerous out of context) is a good warning. Where are the battles in this area being fought today – in private or in relationships?

3. Do you think the essence of the problem in Romans 1:18-27 is wanting to be 'the centre of the universe'? Why does the author think the first commandment – not just the seventh – is crucial? Is he right?

4. The neglect of biblical wisdom going into a relationship (seen in cohabiting couples who adopt the superficial reasons for marrying) plays a heavy part in future pain. What does the author recommend should be followed for better effects? List the priorities.

5. A couple may look good together but what is really different if one belongs to Christ and the other does not? And what is likely to bring tension if one is keen to 'seek first' (Matt. 6:33) and one is not?

6. Where does this chapter get personal, do you think – listening to parents, not being a mummy's boy forever, don't chase boys etc?

7. Who is likely to help the person in church who is too cautious, too cavalier or too conspicuous? Would you leave it to the pastor – or speak up yourself?

8. In all this there is a 'gospel romance' that is more significant and important than all the human relationships. Is this small comfort, or great? (Finish with Rev. 19:5-9 – a better spouse, dress and reception is coming.)

CHAPTER FOUR – THE RELATIONSHIP OF MARRIAGE

1. We know that the submission of Jesus (Phil. 2:5-11) was great and powerful – why does the word 'submit' still sound so annoying when we are told to do it (Eph. 5:21)?

2. It will be good to read again God's big plan (Eph. 1:9-10) and what transformation looks like (Eph. 2:1-10). How realistic is it for the author here to say that 'every relationship [if we belong to Christ] should demonstrate this re-creation harmony'?

3. We tend to think that 'Spirit-filled' (Eph. 5:18) should mean joyful or powerful – what is the shock of 5:18-21 and what does this mean for our behaviour?

4. Restate the wise teaching on how each part in the couplets of Ephesians 5:21-6:9 has the same command but a different expression. Unpack this for each group in a sentence.

5. As a married couple seek to serve God as their primary goal what does male leadership look like in Paul's mind and what does female support look like in Paul's mind? Why are the doctrines of 'creation' and 'redemption' so important in this?

6. How does 'equal but different' work in a team or school, or hospital or government? Could a sense of inferiority creep in here – and what would prevent it?

7. Which parts of the chapter are very searching messages to Christian husbands today and to Christian wives today?

8. Both husband and wife mirror submission to Christ in their submission to one another – do you think refusal of the (vertical) first often causes refusal in the (horizontal) second, while willingness in the first enables willingness in the second?

CHAPTER FIVE – THE RUPTURE OF MARRIAGE

1. Read again (if you haven't lately) 1 Corinthians 7:1-16 to see how compassionate and realistic Paul is about relationship troubles. Are there people in your group who need great love (as well as great truth)?

2. Like praying the first three petitions of the Lord's Prayer, why is 1 Corinthians 7:29-31 so important for perspective on all relationship issues?

3. You can see in 7:10-11 that a separation (for physical or emotional safety) may be necessary but the aim is to reconcile. Jesus has taught against unlawful divorce (Matt. 19:1-9) and– why is 'as long as we both shall live' a good attitude and safeguard?

4. What steps are you aware of that help a couple in trouble to reconcile well? List them.

5. In 7:12-16 the apostle has no quote from Jesus (but speaks with divine authority) to tell believers to stick with their unbelieving spouse. Why might the Corinthians have thought of leaving? Why should Christians today in such a situation be hopeful?

6. 'God's grace has already invaded the household'. Where have you seen God's grace change an unbeliever or strengthen a believer?

7. In 7:15-16 the Christian is 'not bound' to force a relationship that the unbeliever has left. Why is 7:16 (you must not add to the trouble by telling yourself that you are their only hope) a

comfort to many in situations where a loved one is 'away' from the Lord?

8. Grace for repentance, regeneration and restoration. Can we expect a person or couple with a very messy past to be at peace? Is it possible?

CHAPTER SIX – THE REFUSAL, REMOVAL AND RENOUNCEMENT OF MARRIAGE

1. Do you think the church has the balance right in recognising married and single people as 'good' (1 Cor. 7:1-16)? Or do we think more like the world?

2. Better to marry than to burn with the 'shame' of a compromised life (see also Rom. 12:20 for this idea of burning with shame). What should we say to couples who aren't yet married but aren't being godly?

3. 'The whole passage is about contentment'. Why do we always think there is 'greener grass' somewhere else? What is the answer? [see Phil. 4:12 and Phil. 4:13 in context!]

4. Why are so many (who are not committed to serving the Lord as a 'single' person) staying unmarried year after year? Are the men too slow and the women too fussy – and does it matter?

5. The author raises the subject of 'unwanted same-sex attraction'. Why must we make sure that we don't fail them with our 'silence' nor drive them away with our criticism?

6. How helpful is the reminder from older pastors that our sexual struggles – surrendered again and again to Christ – may actually be the very thing that keeps us conscious of His grace and keeps us humble in His service?

7. What is the difference between proud sins and penitent sins? Why is the first so unhelpful and the second so necessary?

8. What did you learn from the Burns poem? How do we follow Jesus (for example, in John 4) by loving the person and still pursuing their salvation through needful steps?

CHAPTER SEVEN – THE PURPOSE OF PARENTHOOD

1. This chapter talks of breathing in the 'air' of secular thinking – especially on why we have children. What does the secular 'air' say about children today and how much has the church absorbed?

2. Have you considered – as first priority for people having children – that they should be bringing up 'the next generation who will continue serving God's kingdom'? How would this reality shape our child-rearing today?

3. Were you raised in the knowledge of God's grace? Why is it essential that children grow up on the backdrop of grace not law? What will be the effect of one or the other? Why is Deuteronomy 6:20-25 so clear on this?

4. Fathers must be physically and 'spiritually present'. Why do you think many fathers fail in this area and what can be done to liberate them to do it?

5. Where have you seen the balance done well of mothers giving priority to their children and also having some work outside the home?

6. The author raises some sensitive issues around couples who think it is wise to refrain from having children. But is the desire to avoid the bother of children (or the risk of children) a dangerous attitude? Why do you think so?

7. How does the distinction between the 'order of nature' and the 'order of creation' help Christians to both trust God and to take action?

8. This issue of children is a church family matter and not just a private decision – how can we create better 'air' on what children are for – in the church context?

CHAPTER EIGHT – THE PURSUIT OF PARENTHOOD

1. This searching chapter helps all Christians to care for the many who have no children or try other avenues to have children. What did you find most helpful in this chapter?

2. Should a couple who 'find themselves unable to have children' ever consider this is part of God's curse? What does Galatians 3:13-14 helpfully teach?

3. Why is affirming the goodness of something that may be denied to a person (marriage or children for example) a help to feeling the grief they may be experiencing?

4. 'None of us can say that we have an absolute right' to children – is this true? Why do we see so much as 'our right' today? [Romans 14 is relevant.]

5. The question for the Christian 'is it right?' is different from the question for the non-Christian 'does it work?'– what does John Wyatt's 'Lego kit' illustration help us to avoid and preserve?

6. What does the 'restoration' principle provide for us as we wrestle with the relevance of science? What biblical passages or principles should we have in mind during our decision making?

7. What are the joys and risks in adoption? What are the joys and risks in IVF?

8. In Matthew 6:25-34 Jesus teaches that we have more than a Creator (of birds and flowers) – we have a Heavenly Father. How should this shape our thinking in the challenges of life and what does 6: 33 promise us?